Manual
of the
Eastern Star

By
Rob Morris, LL. D.
Masonic Writer
1860

This edition by
Cornerstone Book Publishers
Hot Springs Village, AR
2019

Manual of the Eastern Star
by Rob Morris
Foreword by Jonathan K. Poll

A Cornerstone Book
Published by Cornerstone Book Publishers

Copyright © 2019 by Cornerstone Book Publishers

Cornerstone Book Publishers
Hot Springs Village, AR
www.cornerstonepublishers.com

First Cornerstone Edition – 2019

ISBN: 978-1-0882-6264-1

Table of Contents

FOREWORD

This book is a restored reproduction of an invaluable resource written by Rob Morris, the founder of the Eastern Star. This manual can give both practical information, and a historical view on the works of the Eastern Star. Whether you are looking to grow in your participation in the Eastern Star or simply looking for a broader understanding of its works then this book has something for you.

One of the most common criticisms of modern Freemasonry is the exclusion of women from our esoteric works. The history of why this exclusion exists is long, often self-contradictory, and contentious. However, lodges of female Masonry and Mixed-Masonry (men and women) do exist in what is termed "irregular Masonry" or, Masonry not recognized as legitimate in the community of Grand Lodges. But, what exists for women within the recognized community of Freemasonry?

Truly, it is difficult for the wife, or other female relatives of a Mason to properly understand Freemasonry's true significance while only gaining the vaguest glimpses into the deeper workings of a Masonic lodge. This is one of the reasons why Rob Morris created the Eastern Star.

While keeping Freemasonry a male-only fraternity, the Eastern Star can act as a bridge to bring a Mason's family into a Masonic-like atmosphere. The ritual philosophy and traditions of the Eastern Star often reflect those of Freemasonry and can more deeply intertwine a Mason's family into the fraternity.

Many of my own family members are members of the Eastern Star. I can personally see how the influence of this venerable order can bring an Masonic family closer together. The Eastern Star can show us all how to better ourselves and our community.

Jonathan K. Poll
August, 2019

MANUAL
OF THE
EASTERN STAR

DIRECTIONS TO LECTURERS

1. Not less than five ladies form a "Family," or class. It matters not whether a part of these have already received the degrees or not. The only question is, are there five or more ladies present and are they of the proper relationship to the fraternity? As many Master Masons may attend as convenient; the more the better.

2. Unmarried ladies must be eighteen years of age and upwards. Those entitled to this degree are the wives, widows, sisters and daughters of Master Masons, and none other. Stepdaughters, stepsisters and divorced widows are excluded. Moral character must be strictly regarded. Masons' widows who have married persons not Masons are excluded. Daughters and sisters who have married persons not Masons can receive the degrees at the discretion of the Lecturer; but in general it is advised that they should not. All Master Masons in good standing, may and ought to receive it, and become expert in its means of recognition.

3. A secluded apartment must be" secured for conferring the Eastern Star Degree. It is not essential that this should be the Lodge room, although the Lodge room is often the most convenient place that can be found; but a parlor or retired sitting room, or a church in which the blinds can be perfectly closed, is often a more appropriate place for ladies than the Lodge room. But of this, the Lecturer and the ladies themselves are the best judges.

4. To confer the Eastern Star Degree according to this Manual, requires a little over an hour. An hour more, however, can be well spent in explaining the Signet, which every lady should possess, and in practicing upon the signs and passes. No person should aspire to the office of Lecturer until he has

thoroughly qualified himself for the work by imprinting the Lectures upon his memory ; perfecting himself in the signs and passes and Scriptural passages; and securing confidence in himself, so that he may not become confused when he arises to address a class. Do not attempt to confer it without Signets.

5. A class of five or more ladies, seconded by five or more Master Masons, if regularly organized, is styled a "Family," and is expected to hold meetings for work and instruction, at least quarterly. A form of By-Laws will be provided for such.

6. The name and Masonic relationship of every lady to whom this Degree is imparted, must be forwarded to the Grand Patron within one week after the communication.

7. Make the lectures graceful, dignified and impressive. Allow no one to enter the room after the Covenant is imparted. Permit no one to go out of the room. Allow no whispering or confusion during the time of imparting the Degrees. Keep your eye upon the countenance of those to whom you are speaking. It is advised that you confer no other female Degree but this. Stop and rest a few minutes at the end of each half hour, while imparting the Degree.

8. Allow no changes of any sort to be made in the signs, passes or means of recognition, but insist upon a perfect uniformity in all these things.

9. The Eastern Star Degree is not adapted to the Jewish Brethren or their female relatives, though they may receive it if they choose. If any offer to attend, they ought to be informed that it is purely Christian.

MANUAL

Ladies:

We have invited you to meet us today for a double purpose. *First,* that we might take the opportunity to inform you as to your true relationship to the Masonic Fraternity, and thus remove any prejudices you may have entertained against us; and *Second,* to confer upon you, if you wish it, the beautiful, instructive and religious Degree of the Eastern Star. We take it as a compliment to the Freemasons that you have accepted our invitation and come together, and we will endeavor to make this occasion pleasing and instructive to you.

Everybody present knows that Freemasons set a great value upon their mysteries. They put themselves to much trouble and expense to attend their Lodges, and prove by their words and actions that Masonry is deeply implanted in their affections. It must be plain enough to every wife and daughter and sister of a Mason, that there is something in the Lodge, confined to the hearts of the brethren, which is very delightful and precious. To them, and this oftentimes provokes the question, but what use is Masonry to the ladies? As it separates man and wife to some extent, by giving the man certain secrets and duties which the wife cannot share, the ladies sometimes take umbrage against the Society, and even become its enemies and oppose it violently as something contrary to the laws of God and man. A little knowledge, however, of the real nature and purposes of Masonry will remove all this if there is any of it in the minds of the present company.

Masons love and cherish their society above all others, because it makes them better, wiser and happier. *Better,* for it teaches morality, virtue, temperance, economy, charity and justice to all men. *Wiser,* for it imparts knowledge to them that is weighty, solemn and important; knowledge that has been handed down to them from age to age, for nearly three thousand years. *Happier,* for it makes them acquainted and puts them in social connection with the purest and best men in every section of the country. Is it any wonder then, ladies, that Masons love Masonry!

If a Mason is assailed in his character, every other Mason is prompt to defend him, if innocent If he is attacked in person, he finds defenders. If he is distressed for means, poor and in want, being reduced to this by misfortune, his brethren share their abundance wish him. If traveling in a foreign land, he falls sick, or in distress, though all around him may be strangers, the Masons are no strangers to him. They are brothers, and will be as kind to him as though they had known him all his life. If he dies, the Fraternity will bear his body to its last resting place and drop an honest tear to memory, over his remains. Is it any wonder then, ladies, that Masons love Masonry!

But now it is necessary that we should show you why ladies too, should love Masonry, and should be, as many of them are, its warmest friends and defenders. I will answer the question that is often asked, of what use is Masonry to the female sex?

Ladies, you are connected to Masonry by ties far more intimate and tender than you are aware of, or than I can even inform you of. The widow arid orphan daughter of a Master Mason in fact take the place of the husband and father in the affections and good deeds of the Lodge. If their character is unjustly assailed, (and Oh, how often the character of the most virtuous and pure is assailed by the foul tongue of slander!) the brethren will defend them. If they are in want, distressed for the necessities of life, the brethren will divide their means with them. If traveling at a distance from home. they find themselves sick and in want, among strangers, they have but to make themselves known as the widow and the orphan daughter of a worthy Master Mason, and lo, the hand of relief is stretched out toward them! The kind voice of sympathy is heard to cheer them! They are no longer strangers but friends, dear friends, and then they are constrained to bless our society whose kind deeds are not confined to the narrow limits of home.

Ladies, I draw no fancy sketch, I speak of what has happened, of what is happening every day. The widow has been provided with a home, her children educated and reared up to honorable stations, — her own heart cheered and comforted by the blessed influences of Masonry; and this so often in every Lodge in the land, were it our custom to publish abroad such things, a volume would be made up every year of these deeds of heavenly beneficence.

These, then, ladies, are the reasons why we think that you should be the most devoted friends that Masonry possesses. To you is given all the advantages of the society, its shield of protection, its hand of relief and its voice of sympathy,- while we do not require of you any of labor or expense of sustaining it. The only Masonic privilege that is denied to you, is the privilege of visiting the Lodge, and this would be of no advantage to you, even if it were possible. to grant it, but it would awaken the voice of scandal against you from a censorious world, and thus produce far more pain to your kind and virtuous hearts than it could possibly afford you pleasure. Females cannot be made Masons. This is a rule that has been handed down with the other rules of Masonry three thousand years. Each Mason present pledges himself before he is admitted into the Lodge, that he will never allow any of the ancient rules of Masonry to be changed, and this is one of them. Therefore, we cannot invite you to visit our Lodges. But as I have told you, we can and do and will share with you in all the solid privileges and benefits of Masonry and thus practically unite you with us in this great, this glorious, this heavenly work of doing good. Is it any wonder, then, ladies, that we expect you to be the friends of Masonry?

The only objection that can be advanced against what I have said is stated in this question; how is a lady, traveling among strangers, and finding herself in want of friends, to make herself known as the wife, widow, sister or daughter of a Master Mason? Unless she has something more than her mere word to offer, those to whom she applies will be slow to believe her statements. The country is full of imposters, females as well as males. Almost every charitable person has been imposed upon, not once only, but many times. The lady therefore, who can claim the relationship to Masonry that you can, needs, in such a case, some particular means of recognition; some means of making herself known to Master Masons, which no other person would understand; some method, perfect, modest and proper, easily practiced and easily understood. Is there anything of this sort? I imagine you are asking me; is there any means long tried and proved, which a lady can learn and by occasional practice, remember, so that if suddenly called upon, she can put it into use with confidence that it will prove effectual? I answer, there is just such a method, and one principal object of our meeting here today is to teach you that method if you will receive it. The Degree is called the Eastern Star. There are signs and passes and means of recognition which have been tried in a thousand instances and proved to be exactly what a lady needs in the cases I have mentioned. The signs, which are for a lady's use, are easily learned and remembered. The passes which Masons use in answer to the signs are equally so. The other means of recognition by aid of the Signet, which every lady ought to possess, are not easily forgotten; and the whole system is available for practical use when required.

And there is one great merit in the Eastern Star Degree, which if there were no other, would render it worthy of your favor; it is so pure, so graceful and so religious. It gives the history of the heroic daughter of Jephthah, doomed to die for her father's sake. It tells us of Ruth, the harvest gleaner in the field of Boaz, who forsook all things to dwell among the people of God. It speaks of Esther, that noble daughter of bondage who so bravely resolved to share the fortunes of the exiles of Israel. It tells us of Martha, the faithful servant of Christ, mourning the loss of her brother, yet keeping her faith in her Saviour. And finally it thrills us with an account of that devoted Christian, Electa, who above all women suffered for her Master's sake the loss of home, character, family, wealth and life itself.

These are the lessons, ladies, that I offer you in the Eastern Star, if you desire to receive them and nothing more pure or beautiful ever emanated from the human heart than these.

II

But before I dare communicate to you the secrets of the Eastern Star Degrees, whereby you can make yourselves known to Masons, it is necessary that each of you should make a solemn pledge of honor, that these secrets shall be kept honorably in your possession. For any one of you to go out and expose to others what we so secretly tell you here, would not only be fatal to your own character for truth, but would destroy all the advantages of the Degree itself; its great value consists in its being kept in the hands of proper persons. I am happy to inform you that although many thousands of ladies have received it, and they scattered through every section of the country, no instance is on record of any lady having dishonorably exposed it. Nor indeed do we fear that such a misfortune can ever occur. A lady who makes us a pledge of honor, such as I require of you, pledges her very soul; the honor of a woman is more to her than life itself. Those of you, therefore, who give us such security, may safely be trusted with our most cherished secrets.

The pledge we require of you is in this form. I repeat to you now for your consideration. (Repeat it.) If any of you are willing to make so solemn a pledge of honor, you will take the occasion to retire from the room while I address a few words to my Brother Masons.

My Brethren! I have thus far confined my remarks to the ladies, whose coming together today we all feel to be a great compliment to us. You know and can vouch that all my statements as to the principles of Masonry and its advantages to its members are true, and that these ladies do stand in the close relationship to our fraternity that I have described. I will now explain to you that none but the wives, widows, sisters and daughters of Master Masons, and they to be eighteen years and upwards, are entitled to receive the Eastern Star Degrees, and that it must never be conferred unless there are five or more such ladies present. Every Master Mason who will put himself to the trouble of learning the Eastern Star Degree thoroughly, has the same right to confer it that I have, but can only do so under the restrictions I have just mentioned. Each of you must pledge himself to this if you wish to receive it. Please to rise.

So many of you, my brethren, as will pledge the honor of a Master Mason, never to confer or be present at the conferring of the Eastern Star Degree, except under the restrictions mentioned, will raise your right hands. (See that each one does it.) Thank you, Brothers, be seated. (Turn again to the ladies.)

Ladies, I now take it for granted that you who have remained are prepared to give the pledge of honor which I repeated to you. Please to rise.

So many of you, Ladies, as do pledge the sacred honor of a woman never to communicate improperly the secrets of the Eastern Star Degree will raise your right hands. (See that each one does it.) Ladies, I thank you. Be seated. I have no longer any hesitation in saying anything before you concerning this Degree, for I know that my confidence will not be violated.

III

The first thing to which I call your attention is the Signet of the Eastern Star. This is prepared with a view to assist the memory after a person has taken the Degree. It is well called the MONITOR OF THE EASTERN STAR, for by its use you can recall everything that will, today, be communicated to you. And first, observe the five emblems in the center. They are the Open Bible, the Bunch of Lilies, the Sun, the Lamb and the Lion. Each of these, as used here, is a Christian emblem and has a proper motto attached to it.

The Open Bible has its motto at the bottom of the Signet, "The Word of God." The Bunch of Lilies is read on the right, "The Lily of the Valley." The Sun is read at the lower right hand corner, "The Sun of Righteousness." The Lamb is read at the lower left hand corner, "The Lamb of God." The Lion is read on the left, "The Lion of the Tribe of Judah." All these, together with the other mottoes around the sides, "The Bright and Morning Star," "The Star out of Jacob," etc., etc., refer to the Redeemer Jesus Christ, in whom all Christian Masons place their trust and whose birth is alluded to in the sentences at the top. (Give each time to look up the mottoes and let the brethren aid them in doing so.) These emblems will show you how much of religion there is interwoven in this beautiful Degree of the Eastern Star.

You will also remark the Star of the Signet is five pointed. This alludes to the Birth, Death, Resurrection and Ascension of the Lord Jesus Christ. Each point of the Star has a color of its own, the reason of which will be explained to you in due time. The names of the five characters, Jephthah's Daughter, Ruth, Esther, Martha, and Electa are seen in the different points and the histories of these make up the Degree. Each of these has an emblem opposite to it. They are the Sword, the Sheaf, the Crown and Scepter, the Monument. and the Clasped Hands. These form a part of the histories. In fact, without this Signet, it would be as difficult for you to remember the Lectures of the Eastern Star as it would be for the Master Mason to remember the Degrees he learns in the Lodge without his Monitor to refresh his memory.

IV

Should a lady find herself in distress and' among strangers, she may make the acquaintance of any Master Mason who may be present by making one of the five signs which I will now teach you. Each sign has its appropriate sign and explanation, and each has a proper Pass to be given in answer to it by the Mason who recognizes it. I ask your close attention while I teach you these Signs and Passes, as they are the very essence of the Eastern Star Degrees.

The first is called the D. S. or the sign of J. D., and is thus given. (Teach it exactly and practice upon it, explaining the manner of giving it, etc., until all understand it.) When a Master

Mason sees this sign given, it is his duty to respond to it in this way: - he writes his name on a slip of paper and on the back those words, which are the Pass of J.D. This is the introduction between them and enables them safely to go on, and by the other means of recognition to satisfy each other as to their respective Masonic claims. (Repeat the words several times and show the scriptural passages where they may be found; then make the Sign several times and require different gentlemen present to respond in the proper manner. Teach the W. S. or S. of R.; the W. S. or S. of E.; the S. S. or Sign of M. and the C. S. or S. of E. in the same manner. Dwell on each as above. Enlist the ladies in the exercises and require the gentlemen to respond, and thus excite a friendly and pleasing spirit of emulation. But keep all in perfect order. Occupy at least ten minutes on this part of the Lecture.)

V

The origin of these Signs I give you here, and will repeat them again in another part of the Lecture, that you may recollect them the more perfectly. That of J. D. or the D. S. alludes to—. That of R., or the W. S., alludes to—. That of E., or the W. S., alludes to—. That of M., or the S. S., alludes to—. That of E. or the C. S., alludes to—. [In the copy from which this was taken, the secret work was written by hand and inserted in the book.]

JEPHTHAH'S DAUGHTER

The complete history of these five female characters, you will read for yourselves in the Scripture. Doubtless you are already familiar with it I shall, therefore, only give such portions of it as particularly relate to Masonry and the Eastern Star Degree. And I will begin, as the Signet does, with Jephthah's Daughter.

Jephthah was Governor of Israel and commander of the armies of the Lord. He was a pious man, and as our traditions say, a Freemason. Going out on one occasion, at the head of his armies, he prayed most earnestly to God for victory, and made a vow — a rash and unfortunate vow as it afterwards proved — that if his prayer was answered and he should return home in triumph, he would offer as a sacrifice whatever should meet him coming out of his dwelling. His prayer was beard, a splendid victory was given him, and he returned home at the head of his army, rejoicing.

When he arrived at the brow of the hill above his house he paused for a moment, for now he anxiously recalled to his mind his vow, and he waited to see what should first come from his doors. He expected it would be his daughter's pet lamb. But imagine his distress, conceive his anguish and horror when he beheld his daughter, his only child, a fair young maiden just emerging into womanhood, come forth and in the joy of meeting her father run to meet him with singing and dances! He fell on his face in the dust. He rent his clothes, and in the anguish of his heart cried aloud: "Alas, my daughter, thou hast brought me very low!"

When his daughter was informed of his vow, and that her life or his dishonor was its penalty she hesitated not a moment to confirm it. She only said, "My Father, if indeed thou hast opened thy mouth unto the Lord, turn not back." She made but one request, that he would give her two months' time to prepare herself for her terrible fate. It was granted, and she went in company with her female friends, among the caves of the mountains, where they mourned, unceasingly, day and night on account of her impending death.

When the two months had expired, and the day arrived which was to bring this sad affair to a close, a vast multitude gathered together to witness the event. Many thought that Jephthah's daughter would refuse to come and submit to so frightful a doom. But precisely as the sun came on the meridian, she was seen, followed by a long train of her friends, winding their way down the mountain's side to the fatal spot where the altar was erected, and her father, with an almost broken heart, was standing prepared to fulfill his vow.

She approached him, and with one long kiss of affection, bade him farewell. Taking up the thick mourning veil which she had worn, he threw it gently over her face and drew his sword. But she rapidly unveiled herself and said she needed not to have her face covered, for *she was not afraid to die.* Her father replied that he could not strike the blow while she looked upon him, and again cast it over her. She threw it off the second time, and turning from him, said she would look up to the heavens, so that his. hand should not be unnerved by the sight of her face, but that *she would not consent to die in the dark.* A third time, however, he insisted, and a third time she as resolutely cast it off, this time holding it firmly in her hands, and then in the hearing of the multitude, she solemnly declared that if this ceremony was insisted upon she would claim the protection of the law, and refuse the fate that otherwise she was willing to endure. She said it was the practice to cover the faces of murderers ·and criminals when they were about to be put to death, but for her part *she was no criminal and died* only *to redeem her father's honor.* Again she averred that she would cast her eyes upward upon the source of Light, and in that position she invited the fatal blow. It fell. Her gentle spirit mounted to the heavens upon which her last gaze had been fixed, and so the deed was consummated which has rendered the name of Jephthah's Daughter forever famous in the annals of Scripture and of Masonry.

(Here explain again, and carefully, the Sign of Jephthah's Daughter, its origin, application and use. Show too, by the Signet, the application of the Emblem and the Color appropriate to Jephthah's Daughter. The Lecturer should make himself perfectly familiar with the Eleventh Chapter of Judges and especially the extracts given on a subsequent page of this Manual before conferring the Eastern Star Degree.)

RUTH

The Scriptural account of Ruth is one of the most beautiful, tender and touching passages in Holy Writ. It is as interesting to the young as to the old, and opens out to us the most complete account of the usages of ancient society, thirteen hundred years before the coming of Christ, that we possess. But when enlightened by the traditions of Masonry, as given in the Eastern Star Degree, it is still more interesting.

Ruth was of the nation of Moab, a people of idolaters. She married a man of God, by whose pious example and teaching she was converted to the true religion. Upon his death bed he charged her, for her soul's sake, to leave the dangerous company in which she would be thrown, and go to the city of Bethlehem where dwelt the people of God. His name was Mahlon, and our tradition informs us that he was a Freemason.

Immediately after his death she obeyed his pious injunctions. Forsaking her home and friends she journeyed in company with her aged mother-in-law to the land of Israel, and arrived in due time at Bethlehem, but way worn and so poor that she was compelled, for her own support and that. of her friend, to seek some means of securing a livelihood. There was nothing, however, that she could do save to go into the barley fields- for it was the time of harvest, - and glean among the poorest and lowest classes of the people, for a support. The very first attempt she made at this labor exhausted her strength. She had been reared in luxury and the toil was too great for her. The sharp stubble wounded her feet. The blazing sun oppressed her brain. The jeers and insults of her companions alarmed and discouraged her, and long before the hour of noon, with only two little handfuls of barley, as the fruits of her labor, she sought the shade of a tree to refresh herself for a few moments, before retiring from the field.

At this instant Boaz, the owner of the field entered. He was a pious and a charitable man, and as our traditions say, a Freemason. None in Bethlehem was so rich and none 'more beloved than he. As he entered the field, he observed near the gleaners the form of one, differing in garb and manners from the rest, and asked the Overseer who she was? In reply he learned that she was a woman from Moab who asked leave to glean among the sheaves, but that evidently she was unaccustomed to such labor, for she had been there since the sunrise and had gathered but two little handfuls of barley. This excited the kindly feelings of Boaz and he went to her to say a word of sympathy and offer her relief.

As she saw him approach, she supposed him to be the owner of the field and come to order her away as a vagabond or a thief. Ever since the morning she had met nothing but scorn and reproach and she looked for it now. Raising her hands, therefore, to show him how small were her gleanings and that she had stolen nothing from the sheaves, she crossed them meekly upon her breast as showing her willingness to submit to whatever lot she might be called upon to endure, and cast her eyes upward as appealing to God against the inhumanity of man. It was for God she had forsaken home, wealth and friends, and the disconsolate widow, alone in the wide world had none other than He to whom she could look for protection. This mute appeal was not lost upon the kind heart of Boaz. He spoke words of sympathy and tenderness to her. He encouraged her to persevere. From the provisions brought for his reapers he ordered her to eat and drink. He directed ·that handfuls of barley should be dropped on purpose on her way by the reapers, that she might gather an ample supply, so that when she returned to her mother-in-law, she bore with her as much as she would.

The Masonic history of Ruth ends here; but the Scriptural account goes on to say that she became the wife of this generous man and Mason, and that through a long line of posterity, Christ, according to the flesh, was her son. She was the grandmother of Jesse, the father of David, the father of Solomon whose wisdom and might are known equally to every Bible reader and to every intelligent Mason.

To impress upon your memory the Masonic application of the beautiful story of Ruth, I offer you these lines:

From Moab's hills the stranger comes,
By sorrow tried, widowed by death -
She comes to Judah's goodly homes
Led by the trusting hand of faith.

Ye friends of God a welcome lend·
The fair and virtuous Ruth today; -
A generous heart and hand extend
And wipe the widow's tears away.

She leaves her childhood's home and all
That brothers, friends and parents gave ;
The flowery fields, the lordly hall,
The green sod o'er her husband's grave.

Ye friends of God, etc., etc.
She leaves the gods her people own;
Soulless and weak they're hers no more;
JEHOVAH, He is God alone,
And Him her spirit will adore.

Ye friends of God, etc., etc.
At Bethlehem's gates the stranger stands,
All friendless, poor and wanting rest;
She seeks the aid of loving hands
And liberal hearts that God has blessed.
Ye friends of God, etc., etc.

(Here explain again, and carefully, the Sign of Ruth, its origin, application and use. Show too, by the Signet, the application of the Emblem and the Color appropriate to Ruth. The Lecturer should make himself perfectly familiar with the whole Book of Ruth, which is very short, before conferring the Eastern Star Degree.)

ESTHER

The history of Esther is that of a heroine, inspired by the noblest sentiments of religion, to offer her life to save the people of God from destruction. or in the event of failure, to perish with them. The scriptural account of Esther, found in the Book of Esther, is beautiful and instructive; but still more so when enlightened by the traditions of Masonry.

Esther was reared up in obscurity, among the exiled people of Israel, then dwelling in the land of Persia. Her beauty and virtue, and still more, her intellectual endowments attracted the attention of the King, the mighty Ahasuerus, who made her his wife and Queen, presented her with a splendid palace, and honored her above all the women of the land. The more intimate he became with her mental powers the more he admired them. There was no question so difficult she could not aid him to solve; no subject so intricate she could not assist him to unravel. In time he made her his confidant in all the affairs of the kingdom; and in the consideration of every question, she proved herself a true descendant of the wise King Solomon. All the traditions of that period prove that Esther was one of the most remarkable women who ever graced the pages of history.

The traditions of Freemasonry inform us that the King Ahasuerus was a Freemason. He was a man who chiefly valued himself upon keeping his word. The almighty power and importance of truth, was to him, an object of frequent contemplation. You will not be surprised, therefore, when you learn the sequel of this singular history.

The enemies of the Jews, who were very numerous and powerful, had brought the most bitter and false accusations before the King, and had induced him to pass an edict that on a certain day the entire nation should be exterminated. Every man, woman, and child of these unfortunate exiles was to be put to death, and thus the chosen people of God totally blotted out from the earth. But God appointed Queen Esther his instrument to prevent so great a calamity.

No sooner did she learn of this cruel edict, than she resolved to use her influence with the King to save her nation, and if she failed, to perish with them. The King had often promised her that when she came before him robed and adorned as a Queen, and made any request of him whatever, he would grant it, "even to the half of the kingdom." Now was the time to test his sincerity. So devoted to Truth as he was, she could not hesitate to make her appeal to him now. She devoted herself to prayer and fasting for three days and nights, and then causing herself to be attired in the silken robes and with the crown of her royal state, she went boldly through the streets of the city to the palace of the King.

It was a day of state; the King was engaged in giving public reception to the Governors of the many nations under his rule, and his audience-chamber was crowded with the dignitaries of the kingdom. Esther was stopped by the sentinels at the gate and informed that, by a law of the palace, no person, under penalty of death, could enter the King's. presence unless first summoned. Of this, however, she was aware, and passed on, as it were, with her life in her hands.

The scene, as this heroic woman entered the audience-chamber was magnificent. All that could render such an occasion brilliant was there, from the King on this throne, radiant with jewels, to the gorgeous equipage of the officers and decorations of the apartment. In contrast with all this splendid array stood Queen Esther, pale with long fasting and emotion, who strove to catch the eye. of the King. As she did so, he rose, confused and angry that the law of the palace had been violated. At that instant Esther placed her hand upon the crown she wore, and upon the robe, and thus tacitly reminded him of his solemn promise. He remembered his pledge, and calling her to him, at the foot of the throne, held out his golden scepter, that by placing her hand upon it, an evident sign of pardon and acceptance might be seen by all present. Then he said, "What wilt thou, Queen Esther? And what is thy request? It shall be even given thee to the half of the kingdom."

The Masonic history of Queen Esther ends here, but the scriptural account goes on to say that at a proper time she made known her request which was granted by the King, and the whole nation of the Jews was thereby saved. Not one life was sacrificed, and to this day the Jewish people keep one day in each year as a festival to commemorate the boldness, intelligence and fidelity of Queen Esther.

(Here explain again and carefully, the Sign of Esther, its origin, application and use. Show too, by the Signet, the application of the Emblem and the Color appropriate to Esther. The Lecturer should make himself perfectly familiar with the whole Book of Esther, which is not lengthy, before conferring the Eastern Star Degree.)

MARTHA

We come now to those points of the Eastern Star, Martha and Electa, which are particularly of a Christian character, being formed on passages of the New Testament.

The history of Martha is that of a young woman oppressed with grief at the loss of an only brother, yet keeping, amidst death and every discouragement, an unshaken faith in the promises of Christ. Martha and Mary were sisters who dwelt with their brother, Lazarus. The traditions of our Society inform us that he was a Freemason. The three lived together in great harmony, and were favored, above all the citizens of Bethany, by being the friends of Jesus Christ, who, in his frequent visits to the village, made their dwelling his abiding place. They were known by their neighbors as disciples of Him, to whom they showed so many marks of affection.

On one occasion when Christ was absent from Bethany, Lazarus was taken suddenly and violently sick. The case admitted of no delay, the afflicted sisters dispatched a messenger to the place where Christ was, with their wishes expressed in these words, Lord, behold! he whom thou lovest is sick! They might well have thought that such an appeal would have brought their Divine Friend to their aid in the greatest haste, and that the life of Lazarus might thus be saved. But though the messenger returned, Jesus did not come. Lazarus grew worse, while the sisters listened for the feet of their expected guest, - and died. He was taken immediately to the sepulcher, according to the custom of the country, and those morning females felt they were alone. Their brother dead. Their friend, upon whose miraculous power they had relied so greatly, deserter in their greatest time of need. What had they to live for now?

But Christ, though apparently negligent to their call, knew better than they themselves what was best for them. He was but trying their faith and that dead man, sleeping in his gloomy sepulchre, was a part of the trial. At the end of the fourth day, Martha, who had never ceased to look towards Jerusalem, with a half-hope that he would yet come and bring peace to their wounded hearts, heard the message, the Master is coming, and ran eagerly to the edge of the village to greet him. She fell on her knees before him, and with her hands upraised in an attitude of supplication, and in soft and loving words rebuked the tardiness which had cost her brother's life. Looking into his face she saw the gentle smile there which always spoke of hope and mercy, and was constrained to add, "But I know that even now, whatsoever thou wilt ask of God, God will give it thee."

Jesus saith unto her, "Thy brother shall. rise again."

Martha said unto him, "I know that he shall rise again in the resurrection, at the last day."

Jesus saith unto her, "I am the resurrection and the life; he that believeth in me, though he were dead, yet shall he live; and whosoever liveth and believeth in me shall never die. Believest thou this?"

Thus the Saviour tried the faith of Martha. Did she believe that He had the power, then and there, to raise her brother from the dead? That was the meaning of his question. It would have proved a hard one to others, but not to her. She answered at once, in the tone and spirit of perfect faith, "Yea Lord, I believe that thou art the Christ, the Son of God, which should come unto the world!"

The reward of such faith was soon rendered. Taking her by the hand and passing by their dwelling, where they were joined by Mary, they went to the sepulchre, and as every scripture reader knows, Jesus raised the dead man to life.

(Here explain again, and carefully, the Sign of Martha, its origin, application and use. Show too, by the Signet, the application of the Emblem and the Color appropriate to Martha. The Lecturer should make himself perfectly familiar with the Eleventh Chapter of John, before conferring the Eastern Star Degree.)

ELECTA

The last of these five female characters, whose virtues and misfortunes make up the glory of the Eastern Star, is Electa. No account of this celebrated woman is given in the scriptures; we are entirely indebted for what we know of her, to Masonic tradition. Her husband's name was Gaius, and he was long Grand Master of Masons, in which situation he was succeeded by the illustrious John, the Evangelist. Electa had been reared up among a heathen people, and like the rest had been taught to worship idols, in which faith she had reared her children. But happening by good chance to hear a discourse from the Christian missionary, Paul, she with her husband and all their family, yielded their faith to Him whose gospel was so powerfully imparted to them, and they became Christians. It was at a period when all manner of persecution awaited those who professed the Christian faith. Imprisonment., scourgings, loss of property and often the loss of life was the price paid by those who gave in their adhesion to Christ Electa and her family, however, were spared for many years. The Masonic influence which her husband so largely shared, made friends amongst those who would otherwise have persecuted them; and although. they were often scorned and pointed at as the followers of a crucified Saviour, yet no other evil befell them.

In adopting the Christian religion, Electa had adopted all the virtues and graces that flow out of it. To spend her large income in relieving the poor; to devote much of her time to the care of the sick; to keep an open house for indigent and hungry travelers- these were among the least of the good deeds which the spirit of Christ's religion taught her to perform. She was ripening daily for a better world. Her children growing around her, were her's as well by faith in Christ as by the ties of blood.

Her fame went everywhere as Electa, the mother of the faithful, the friend of the distressed.

But now the time of trial came. Strict orders were issued from the Roman Emperor that all who professed the name of Christ should recant or suffer death. The soldiers swept through the land in search of all those who were known as being of this faith, and thousands in every part suffered martyrdom for their fidelity to the cause. It was riot possible that so shining a mark as Electa should escape, and a band of soldiers soon found their way through those doors so long opened for the entrance of the poor and distressed. But the captain of the band was a Freemason, and most loth to injure one of whose good deeds he had heard so much. He besought her therefore, ardently, to recant from Christianity. He told her the recantation was a mere form, which need not indeed affect her private opinions and handed her a Cross which he bade her throw upon the floor and put her foot upon it, assuring her that he would then leave her without danger, and make report that she had recanted. ·

She took the Cross, but it was to press it to her bosom, to her lips, to weep tears of love to Christ upon it, to assure the soldier that in this sign she was more than willing· to die, and that from the hour she professed the Christian religion, she had waited eagerly for this opportunity to testify her love for Christ. She told him to do his duty, whatever it was, and Christ would give her Divine Grace to do hers. The family was then cast into a loathsome dungeon where they remained for a year. Their splendid dwelling was then burned to ashes and all their property taken away or destroyed. They were reduced to want in a single day. At the end of the year the Roman Judge came in person to their cell and being also a Freemason, and one who had often sat lovingly under the instruction of the Grand

Master, her husband, besought them yet, as it was not too late, to save their lives by recanting from their faith. He pleaded with them by many arguments, by their love for their children, by the love of life and by the horrors of the death which infallibly awaited them if they persisted in their determination, to yield ere it was too late. But Electa made answer as before and so did all her family. It was good, she said, that they for whom Christ died, should give testimony to the power of his death, by dying for him.

Then came the last sad scene. They were taken from the dungeon and savagely scourged, mother, father and children, until life barely lingered in their tortured bodies. Then they were taken in carts drawn by oxen, amidst the jeers and scorn of the people, to the nearest hill and one by one nailed to crosses. As the meek and loving servant of Christ was left until the last she saw her husband and children suspended until speedy death released them from their sufferings. Then came her turn and she soon gave up her spirit to God, her last words being a prayer for pardon upon her guilty murderers.

In the next Grand Lodge St. John related her history and as there were few present who had not shared in her kindness and hospitality, the relation was received with profound interest. At his suggestion the whole was agreed to be perpetuated by sign and pass as I have given them to you, and so for 1800 years one generation to another has told the mournful yet triumphant story of the Christian martyr, Electa.

(Here explain again and carefully, the Sign of Electa, its origin, application and use. Show too, by the Signet, the application of the Emblem and the Color appropriate to Electa.)

VII

Thus I have completed these five beautiful histories and you can readily perceive by them how instructive are the Masonic traditions, when applied as they should be, to the Scriptures. I again call your attention to the Signet of the Eastern Star that I may explain to you the [Cabalistic motto]. Jephthah's Daughter, because she cheerfully rendered up her life to preserve her father's honor was --. Ruth because she forsook home, friends and wealth that she might dwell among the people of god was --. Esther because she was prepared to resign her crown and life to save the people of God from death or perish with them was --. Martha because amidst sickness, death and loneliness she never for a moment doubted the Saviour's power to raise the dead was --. And finally Electa, because she joyfully rendered up her home, husband, children, good name and life that she might testify to her Christian love by a martyr's death, was--. So, ladies, let it be with each of you. As you illustrate the virtues of these chosen and tried servants of God, so shall be your reward. You will not be called to suffer as they did, and yet sufferings and trials do await all of us in this sublunary state; and those who in the place to which they are called best endure these trials and resist temptations prove that, had they lived in the ancient times, they would not have been found wanting though called to endure as a Ruth or as an Electa.

One word more. As Freemasons, we earnestly solicit your good will and encouragement in the work in which we are engaged. I have proved to you that it is for your good as much as ours that we are doing the Masonic work. Then, ladies, help us. Help us by defending our principles when you hear them attacked, and speaking ever a kind word in our behalf. Your smile and favor are the best encouragement we seek; with them we can do everything, and with them we pledge ourselves to do a double portion for you. And to those kind ladies who thus, while living, prove themselves the friends of Masons and of Masonry, we promise that living we will love and respect you, and when you pass from this world to a better we will remember you as — .

Scripture Extracts

For Jephthah's Daughter, Judges II, 29-40
For Ruth and Naomi, Ruth II, 1-17
For Esther, Esther V, 1-8
For Martha, St. John II, 1-44
For Electa, The Second Epistle of John 1-13

BOOK OF INSTRUCTIONS

Chapter First

Organizing the "F".

Section 1

Preparatory to the organization of a F., the Patron should take a careful, deliberate and thorough survey of his intended field of operations, weigh the circumstances to be met, the obstacles to be encountered, and the advantages to be anticipated. No two localities present the same peculiarities; and it is therefore impossible for me to offer rules or special advice for your direction here; but, in general, I would say, that if any considerable number of the members of your Lodge are opposed to the attempt, or if the ladies and friends of Adoptive Masonry live too far apart for regular meetings (monthly or quarterly), it is best not to organize a F. at first, but confine yourself to conferring the E. S. in the plain and quiet manner described in the Manual, until you have overcome the worst prejudices, and enlarged the circle of the friends of the cause.

After a careful estimate I have come to this conclusion, that with three-fourths of the Lodges of this country, there may and ought to be a F. established, one for each; and that where as many as ten ladies can be found who will regularly unite in the meetings of a F., there is ample encouragement to establish and continue one. The advantages derived from them are:

First — The cultivation of a social spirit among the members. In country localities this is eminently desirable.

Second — The relief of the distresses of the poor and destitute. In towns and villages this is eminently desirable.

Third — The communication of interesting and important truths, which have their foundation in the Word of God, to those ladies who from their relationship by blood or marriage with Master Masons, are entitled to receive them.

Fourth - The brightening and strengthening of the golden links of affection which bind true and loving hearts together in the spirit of Jesus Christ. These are just and noble aims.

SECTION 2

The Charter, Membership Board, By-Laws, and Book of Instructions being received, the Patron proceeds to organize the F. according to the following forms:

Due announcement of the time and place of meeting must be made to each of the signers 'of the Petition. The *time* should be by daylight, except in towns and villages, where the night may be more convenient, and the *place* either at the Masonic Hall or at some private apartment, at the discretion of the Patron. Be careful in all your doings to consider delicacy and propriety, as well as caution and circumspection.

No persons are allowed to be present at the organization of a F., except those whose names are appended to the original petition. But in cases of emergency, the Patron is authorized, by the unanimous consent of the petitioners present, to add other names sufficient to make the number *ten,* so as to proceed with the organization; and in that event, all the ladies and gentlemen present at the organization, will be considered as *the original members of the F.*

SECTION 3

The petitioners being thus duly met and proper precautions having been taken against spies and intruders, the proceedings are opened by the Patron appointing temporarily all the officers of the F., himself acting as PATRON. Then he calls by name, upon each one present, beginning with the gentlemen, and makes the following inquiry:

Do you agree upon your honor that you will abide by the Regulations of this Order as embraced in these By-Laws, and conform to all the lawful rules of this F., so long as you may remain a member thereof? *Each one must answer, I do, and make the Hailing Sign of Electa, in confirmation thereof.*

Then the Patron will read a portion of the 84th Psalm as follows:

How amiable are thy tabernacles, O Lord of hosts!

My soul longeth, yea, even fainteth for the courts of the Lord: my heart and my flesh crieth out for the living God.

Blessed are they that dwell in thy house: they will be still praising thee.

Blessed is the man whose strength is in thee; in whose heart are the ways of them.

Who passing through the valley of Baca, make it a well; the rain also filleth the pools.

They go from strength to strength; every one of them in Zion appeareth before God.

For a day in thy courts is better than a thousand. I had rather be a door-keeper in the house of my God, than to dwell in the tents of wickedness.

For the Lord God is a sun and shield. The Lord will give grace and glory. No good thing will he withhold from them that walk uprightly.

O Lord of hosts, blessed is the man that trusteth in thee.

All present will then unite in singing the following

ODE

O, that in this world of weeping,
Widow's tears and orphan's cry,
Hearts their term of trial keeping,
Would but melt in sympathy!

O, that we, each Sister, Brother,
Traveling on the self same road,
In our love for one another,
Would but love the love of God!

For that love would surely teach us
Ne'er to crush a burdened heart,
By the tender thoughts that reach us
When we see a tear drop start;

And the lonely, poor and saddened,
In their almost cheerless grief,
By our liberal bounty gladdened,
Would acknowledge the relief.

Here, then, met in social pleasure,
Here before the Word Divine,
While our life contains the treasure,
Let us in this covenant join –

Tears to dry, to comfort sighing,
Gentle words and smiles to strew–
By the sick and by the dying,
Patient, God-like love to show.

Then, though we must part like others,
And the dead be joined among,
In the hearts of Sisters, Brothers,
We shall be remembered long.

Those who speak of us shall name
As the dead to memory dear,
And the page of friendship claim us
Worthy of a grateful tear.

A prayer is then offered by the Patron or by someone deputed by him, for that purpose, as follows:

Source of all Wisdom, Truth and Love: grant to us that in the establishing of the Society we may add strength to our strength and grace to our grace. May the golden links thus lengthened, become the brighter for the links we are now adding to them, and be strengthened for the great work we have to do. Enlarge our powers to benefit mankind and to honor Thee; and one by one each link shall fall away in death, may the parting be temporary, but the meeting eternal. And in the world to come where death enters not, may we realize the full happiness of loving Thee and serving Thee forever. We ask through Christ the Saviour. Amen.

Section 4

The Patron then delivers an address appropriate to the occasion, in which he enlarges upon the objects sought for in the organization of the F., and encourages the audience by relating the advantages derived by others from efforts of this sort. He points out to them the importance of prompt and regular attendance upon the meetings of the F., and exhorts them to be faithful in the performance of the duties inculcated by this Order. He shows them that as the principal advantages of Masonry are derived from its *principles of association,* so the main advantage of this Order consists in *its meetings* and the pleasant acquaintances formed and cemented therein. He explains particularly how a member of this F. is equally welcomed and adopted in every other F. wherever established, and extols this as one of the highest encomiums that can be pronounced upon the Masonic and Adoptive systems. Finally he pledges, on his own part, an earnest advocacy of this Order, and promises to give regular and unremitting attention to its interests, so far as they are connected with the F. now organized.

The Patron is at liberty to select any other member, in his own discretion, to deliver the opening address in his stead.

SECTION 5

The Patron now communicates the SOCIAL GRIP and COUNTERSIGN to the Patroness, and she to the other ladies. The Patron then communicates the SOCIAL GRIP and COUNTERSIGN to the gentlemen. (See Appendix for the Social Grip and Countersign.)

SECTION 6

The Membership Board is now filled out by the Recorder in the following manner: The names of the ladies are first written upon the rays or lines drawn from the center to the circumference of the Membership Board, beginning with the ray numbered "1. Affection," and going around with the numbers. One name is written upon each ray, upon the *under* side of it, about half way from the center to the circumference, thus, "Mary A. Carneal," in plain, round hand, taking great pains to spell each name correctly.

This being done, write in the broad part of the ray, near the center of the picture, the *class of ladies* to which each lady belongs, viz.: "Wife," "Widow," "Sister," or "Daughter," in plain round hand.

Should the gentleman be dead through whom a lady was first Adopted, his name should nevertheless be inserted, for this is the record of her privileges as an adopted Sister in Masonry. Should the lady change her condition from "Sister" to "Wife" or from "Daughter" to "Wife," etc., the name of the gentleman first written may be erased, and another one inserted if she so desires it, or the original entry may stand, according to her own choice. As new names are added to the Membership Board, the same rule is followed, and when the twenty-five rays are filled up, additional names to any extent. may be written above and below the original ones. No name can lawfully be added to the Membership Board except *in open Family,* and by the express order of the Family.

As members whose names have been enrolled, die, withdraw, remove from the jurisdiction, or are suspended, their names on the Membership Board must be enclosed in brackets, and the date of their death, withdrawal, removal, or suspension be appended.

SECTION 7

The next step in the organization of the Family, is the selection of appropriate flowers by the ladies for their respective emblems, and their record upon the Membership

Board. For the proper method of selection, etc., see Chapter Third, on the "Reception of Members."

Section 8

The Patron then announces as follows :

In the name of Adoptive Masonry at large, and by the authority invested in me, in this Charter, I now declare .... Family No. . . . . duly organized and empowered to work as a regular Family of the Eastern Star.

A notification of this should be made as early as possible to the Grand Patron.

Section 9

The election of Patron and Treasurer for the ensuing year is then had. This must be done by secret written ballot, in which each lady and gentleman is allowed one written vote. But no Brother can serve as Patron who is not already enrolled as a Patron of the E. S. upon the books of the Grand Patron. The election being completed, the Patron appoints the Patroness, and they jointly appoint the remaining officers, to hold office until the ensuing New Year's Day, or until their successors are duly elected and installed.

Section 10

The officers, whether elected or appointed, are then installed as follows: each one rising, raising the right hand, the Patron pronounces this form of covenant:

You and each of you do pledge your sacred honor, in the presence of this FAMILY, that you will perform the duties of the office to which you have been elected or appointed, to the utmost of your zeal and fidelity.

To this each officer replies audibly: I do, upon my honor.

SECTION 11

As the Charter sent to the Family contains many blanks, these should be filled out by the Recorder under the direction of the Patron as follows:

The name of the Patroness should be inserted opposite "LUNA."

The name of the Conductor should be inserted opposite "PHILOMATH."

The name of the Conductress should be inserted opposite "FLORA."

The name of the Treasurer should be inserted opposite "VERGER."

The name of the Recorder should be inserted opposite "HERALD."

The name of the Watchman should be inserted opposite "WARDER."

The three other blanks, viz.: "HEBE," "THESIS," and AREME" must be filled by the three petitioners whose names have not been used as above.

The Recorder of the Family is authorized to sign his name as Grand Secretary at the bottom of the Charter, adding p. t. (pro. tempore) to his signature. The use of the old form of Charter is continued, although the Association governed by the Supreme Constellation has ceased to exist. This is done to show that the two systems of "Constellations" and "Families" are identical in spirit, the latter having taken the place of the former. It serves further to show that the thousands of ladies who were introduced to the advantages of Adoptive Masonry under the former system, retain their privileges under the latter.

The business of the Family is then taken up as described in Article 2d, Section 2, of the By-Laws, except that the first specification may be omitted as the F. is already opened. For the manner of conferring the Degree of E. S., receiving new members into the Family and holding the Banquet, see the appropriate Chapters in this Book of Instructions.

SECTION 12

The following system of signals applies to all the ceremonies of the Family:

1. Signal to be seated and keep silence: I-I-I-I-I.
2. Signal to rise to feet : II-I-I-I.
3. Signal that the Family is opened: III-I- I.
4. Signal that a candidate is without: IIII-I.
5. Signal that the Family is about to close: I-II-II.

These signals are made with a spring bell, or by clapping the hands smartly together at intervals of one-half second and one second, according to the distances indicated in the print.

CHAPTER SECOND

OPENING AND CLOSING THE FAMILY

SECTION 1

Punctuality in opening the F. at the time indicated in the By-Laws, is highly essential, and to this the Patron is earnestly enjoined. The hall or room chosen for the family meetings should be carefully swept and garnished with flowers, wild and cultivated; or in winter seasons artificial. These must represent Violets, Heliotropes (Sunflowers), White Lilies, Pine Sprigs, and Red Roses. Any other flowers, however, having the same colors, will serve as a proper substitute. The Sisters are expected to wear, at the meetings of the Family, small bouquets in their headdress; the gentlemen the same in the center buttonhole of the coat, on the left side. These may be natural or artificial, as the exigencies of the case demand.

A spring bell will be found highly convenient in giving the various SIGNALS, but is not essential. A copy of the Holy Scriptures, the CHARTER, MEMBERSHIP BOARD, BY-LAWS, and BOOK OF INSTRUCTIONS, are indispensable as the furniture of the family.

SECTION 2

The Regalia or Badges are as described in Article 7, Section 2 of the By-Laws, but for the first meeting of the Family it will be sufficient to provide pieces of broad white ribbon with a red five pointed star (the size of a half dollar), sewed or embroidered on each. This to be worn about the left arm at the elbow by each lady and gentleman of the Family. The other regalia may be prepared as soon as convenient, viz.: the Apron, Gloves, and Collar for each lady. The gentlemen wear no badges save the bouquets and the fillet about the left elbow.

SECTION 3

The ceremony of opening the Family at a Stated Meeting is thus performed: The Patron observing that at least five ladies and five gentlemen are present (including himself), and that the Charter, Membership Board, etc., are at hand, stations the Watchman in such a position as to guard against espionage or intrusion. He may be within or without the door at his own convenience. If any of the officers are not present, the Patron appoints members to fill the vacancies.

Taking his own seat at the end of the room, opposite the principal door of entrance, he seats the Patroness on his left, the Treasurer on his right a little in front, and the Recorder on his left a little in front.

He then directs the Conductor to place himself at the end of the room opposite to him, the Conductress seating herself on the right of the Conductor. This brings the Patron and Conductor (also the Patroness and Conductress), directly opposite to and facing each other.

On a table at the right hand of the Patron, lie the Charter and Membership Board. If, however, these objects have been framed, they should be suspended on the wall, immediately behind the chair of the Patron. On a table at the left hand of the Conductor, lie the Bible and By-Laws of the Family. The spring bell, if the Family have one, is on the Patron's table. The Patron must have a desk or table for his use.

Selections from the Scriptures are then read by the Patron. These consist of such portions of Holy Writ as may be preferred by him; but it is recommended that passages be selected which refer to the histories of Jephthah's Daughter, Ruth, Esther and Martha; also the more pathetic passages from the Gospels, such as the Raising of the Son of the Widow of Nain, Christ's Agony in the Garden, Christ blessing little children, the Crucifixion, etc., etc. The amount of matter to be read is subject to the discretion of the Patron.

The Family is then called by the signal from the Patron, and an ode is sung. This is one of the seven odes found in the appendix to the By-Laws; or any other appropriate ode may be selected at the discretion of the Patroness. If there are members belonging to the Family who possess poetic genius, it. will be highly appropriate to use original odes written by them.

A prayer is now offered by the Conductor. The following form of prayer may be used, or any other appropriate form at the Conductor's discretion. The Conductor is also at liberty to offer up an extemporaneous prayer, or to request some other member to do so if he prefer it.

Oh! Thou who didst inspire holy men and women in ancient times, to show forth examples of self-sacrifice, faith and devotion, inspire us who have now assembled together to like deeds of worthiness. May we sympathize in the cares and sufferings of each other. May we have a tender sympathy for the sorrows of the poor and afflicted. May all our actions be shaped by the precepts thou hast given us in the Holy Word, that so, when our life of labor is ended, we may be accepted into the family of the Redeemed. We ask through Jesus Christ, the Saviour, Amen.

The Hailing Signs of the five Degrees of the Eastern Star are then given with accuracy and precision, all the members looking to the Patron and taking the movements from him.

After this the FAMILY HAIL is given, commencing with the Patron and followed in succession by the Patroness, Conductor, Conductress, Treasurer, Recorder, and Watchman. The gentlemen then approach the Patron one by one, and give him the SOCIAL GRIP and COUNTERSIGN. The ladies in like manner approach the Patroness and give her the SOCIAL GRIP AND COUNTERSIGN.

The Patron then makes the following announcement, viz.:

I declare .... Family, No . ... , now open according to the forms of the Order. And I solemnly enjoin upon all here assembled to remember the purposes for which the family was constituted and the high principles inculcated in our Order. Remember JEPHTHAH'S DAUGHTER, who cheerfully rendered up her life to preserve her father's honor; and RUTH, who forsook home, friends and wealth, that she might dwell among the people of God; and ESTHER, who was ready to resign her crown and life to save the people of God, or perish with them; and MARTHA, who amidst sickness, loneliness and death, never for a moment doubted the Saviour's power to raise the dead; and ELECTA, who joyfully surrendered home, husband, children, good name and life, that she might testify her Christian love by a martyr's death. Remember these, and strive like them, to be worthy of the appellation, * * * * * * *

The Patron then makes the signal to be seated. The Conductor goes without further direction to the Watchman and announces to him that the Family is opened. This completes the ceremony of OPENING.

The order of business at a stated meeting is:

1. Rehearsing the Lectures.
2. Delivery of Essays.
3. Banquet.

4. Closing Ceremony.

SECTION 4

The ceremony of CLOSING is brief and simple. The order of business being conducted according to the By-Laws, Article 2nd, Section 2, the Patron announces his intention to close the Family. The signal for rising is then given, and an appropriate ode, selected by the Patroness, is sung.

The Hailing Signs of the five Degrees of the Eastern Star, are then given, also the FAMILY HAIL., SOCIAL. GRIP and COUNTERSIGN, as at the OPENING. The Patron then makes the following announcement:

I declare Family No. .... now closed according to the forms of the Order and I solemnly charge all present to carry with you at your departure, the sacred and inspiring lessons that have been here inculcated, and let them abide and become fruitful in your hearts. Be patient, be charitable. Exercise the spirit of friendship to all, and trust hopefully in God. That so, if we do not meet again in the Family on earth, we may have happy seats in the Family above, whose ruler, light and bounteous reward is the Lord Jesus Christ Amen.

The Conductor then announces to the Watchman that the Family is closed and all disperse.

CHAPTER THIRD

RECEPTION OF MEMBERS

SECTION 1

The Family being regularly opened according to the directions contained in the last Chapter, the first business in order is to rehearse the Lectures with accuracy and completeness. This includes the conferring of the Degrees of the E. S. upon candidates, if any are in waiting, who have been approved by the Patron and Patroness.

To prepare the Family for conferring the Degree of the E. S., the Patron announces as follows :

I declare .... Family, No ...., now in order, for the reception of candidates for the Degree of the Eastern Star.

The object of this announcement is, that strangers may be admitted into the Family without giving them an opportunity of witnessing the peculiar ceremonies as described in Section .... The announcement is also a caution to the members present, to make no signs, passes, etc., while the visitors are in the Family.

This announcement having been made, the visitors being previously vouched for, and accepted by the Patron and Patroness, are admitted without ceremony, by the Watchman, introduced by the Conductor to the members of the Family, and conducted to appropriate seats. Then the Patron proceeds at once to confer the Degree, according to the directions given in the "Manual of the Eastern Star."

The manner of conferring the Degree of E. S. within the Family, is the same as within a private convocation. To confer it properly requires a little over an hour. The Patron should be thoroughly qualified and have the Lectures as given in the Manual, imprinted upon his memory. He should be perfect in the signs, passes and scriptural passages. The Lectures should be given in a graceful, dignified and impressive manner. No one should be permitted to retire during their rehearsal, except in cases of emergency, nor then save by permission from the Conductor.

The members of the Family are not under compulsion to admit to membership those upon whom they confer the Degree E. S. On the contrary, it will often occur, that Ladies and Masons from other Lodges, will attend the meetings of the Family for the sake of acquiring the Degree of E. S., who from distance, or other circumstances, would not be desirable members of the Family. It is entirely proper and it is recommended, that the Family should by vote, charge a small fee for conferring the Degree under the circumstances named above.

The name of all ladies and gentlemen receiving the Degree in the Family as above, must be entered upon the records by the Recorder, and certified lists be forwarded to the Grand Patron.

No action of the Family is required upon a proposition to *confer the Degree of E. S.,* as that is a matter left entirely in the option of the Patron. Yet should a member of the F. positively object to *it being conferred in the F.,* upon any particular applicant, the Patron must respect the objection, and forbear to confer it upon the applicant.

But where the applicant desires *both to receive the Degree of E. S. and to become a member of the F.,* the following form of petition must be used, viz.:

To the officers and members of Family............... No.........:

The undersigned respectfully petitions to receive the Degree of the Eastern Star, and to become a member of your Family. If approved, she (he) pledges herself (himself) to a cheerful obedience to all the requirements of the Society and the Family.

(Date)   (One recommender)   (Name)

This petition must be accompanied by the fee, as designated by the By-Laws of the F. The petition must be given by the Secretary to the Patron if the applicant is a male, or to the Patroness if the applicant is a female. The Patron and Patroness will then consult together upon the propriety of accepting the applicant, taking much counsel from the other members of the F., as they may deem necessary to promote harmony and good feeling. If rejected, the fees must be returned to the applicant.

SECTION 2

The petition having been duly considered and accepted as above, the manner of initiating an applicant into membership of the F. is as described below.

The Conducting is performed by the Conductress, if applicant is a female; by the Conductor if applicant is a male. Each officer should endeavor to throw an air of seriousness and impressiveness about the language and ceremonies. The particular part of each officer may be drawn off, in writing, from this BOOK OF INSTRUCTIONS, and used to guide the memory, though it is far better that each should commit the whole of her (or his) part to memory so perfectly as to need no aid of that sort.

The applicant being announced at the door by the Watchman, the Conductress, if the applicant is a female, goes out and conducts her in, leading her by the left hand. No special form of words or ceremony are used in this part of the introduction. The Conductress leads her directly in front of the Patron, and introduces her as follows:

Enlightened Patron: It becomes my pleasant duty to introduce to you our Sister in Adoptive Masonry, Mrs. (or Miss) A-B-. This lady has received the Degree of the Eastern Star, having first made an inviolable pledge of secrecy according to our rules. She has heard with emotion, the painful yet glorious history of Jephthah's daughter; she has contemplated the noble self-devotion of Ruth and Esther; she has witnessed the tears of the faithful Martha, and has paid the tribute of her own generous sympathy to the martyrdom of the Christian Electa; she desires now to make one of this Family of the Eastern Star, where such histories are studied and such virtues emulated, and she has entered amongst us, determined to bear her part in this good work.

To this introduction the Patron responds by making the signal for all to rise, and thus addressing the candidate:

My Sister, we hail with unaffected pleasure your coming amongst us. The work of Adoptive Masonry is amply broad enough for us all, and we shall rejoice to find you excelling in your zeal and devotion the most active members of our Order.

We are laboring to increase our own happiness by promoting the good of others. Our experience and the wisdom gained from the Holy Writings alike teach us that this world is a harsh, unfriendly scene, poorly adapted to impart happiness, and that it is chiefly by combining the efforts of the good and true in the work of morality and religion that happiness is to be acquired and extended. The greater our ability to do good, the more happiness we shall enjoy.

We meet in private. This is so that we may arrange our plans for the good work in which we are employed, without interruption from those who could not understand or sympathize with us. In our meetings, we strive to learn our duties as beings who possess immortal spirits, and when we return home we make it our earnest care to perform those duties. We cultivate a spirit of harmony in order 'that the enemy of our souls may acquire no advantage over us.

And as a large portion of our work as Adoptive Masons consists in acquiring the work and temper of Jesus Christ, whom to know is everlasting life, we often unite in addressing the Heavenly Throne and pleading with God, that the very spirit of faith and wisdom may descend upon us, and make our place of meeting a Bethel, where the Divine Spirit shall be pleased to dwell. It is expected that you will now signify your assent to three propositions.

First - Are you a believer in the doctrines of the Old and New Testament?

Answer. - *I am.*

Second - Do you pledge yourself in the presence of this Family, to conform to its By-Laws and Rules so long as you remain a member of it?

Answer. - *I do.*

Third - Should you ever withdraw from the membership of the Family will you always keep secret whatever you may see and hear of its proceedings while a member?

Answer. - I will.

The Patron then addresses the members of the Family as follows:

Sisters and *Brethren:* You have heard with what cheerful readiness this lady has assented to the propositions made to her. Such a disposition promises well for her usefulness as a member

of the Family. Her high standing in virtue, honor and sincerity permits no room for doubt that she will do all that she has promised. You will therefore be expected to signify your assent to two propositions.

First. Do you still consent to this lady, Mrs. (or Miss) A-------B-------, becoming a member of this Family?

Each one answers, *I do.*

Second. Will you endeavor by all proper methods to render her position as a member of this Family, pleasant and useful to her?

Each one answers, *I will.*

The Patron then addresses the candidate as follows: My Sister, the covenant between you and the members of this Family, having been established by these mutual reciprocal pledges, I now declare you to be a member in full standing of .... Family, No. .... , and entitled to all its honors and privileges. Behold the FAMILY HAIL or acclamation by which the members of a Family address and recognize each other.

The Patron now makes the Family Hail, in which he is followed by all the members of the Family, and then by the newly admitted Sister. Its origin and the manner of using are also explained.

The Patron addresses the Patroness as follows: *Enlightened Patroness,* Sister A-------

B------- having been regularly admitted as a member of this Family, it devolves upon you to bestow upon her the Social Grip.

The Patroness communicates to her the SOCIAL GRIP, shows its origin and practical use. Then the Patron addresses the Conductress as follows: *Respected Conductress,* Sister A------B------ having been instructed in the FAMILY HAIL and SOCIAL GRIP, it now devolves upon you to impart to her the COUNTERSIGN of this Family.

The Conductress then takes the newly admitted Sister by the SOCIAL GRIP and pronounces the COUNTERSIGN audibly.

The Patron then addresses the Recorder as follows: *Respected Recorder,* Sister A------- B------- having made all the pledges, and satisfied all the requirements of this Order and Family, you will record her name upon the Membership Board, as a Sister in full fellowship with us.

The Recorder obeys as directed in Chapter I, Section 6, and the newly admitted Sister takes her seat on the right of the Patron. This completes the ceremony of receiving a member.

If the applicant is a male instead of a female, the Conductor will take the place and perform the duties as described in this section. A few verbal changes must be made in the introduction. The SOCIAL GRIP in this case will be made by the Patron and the COUNTERSIGN by the Conductor. The candidate, if a male, is conducted by the right hand instead of the left, and when admitted and enrolled, he takes his seat on the right of the Conductor.

SECTION 3

Every female member of the F. is required to select an Emblem within three months of her admission to the F., but the best time for this is at the time of her admission. The Recorder is required to keep a book in which the Emblems are recorded. The method of selection is as follows:

The Patron addresses the newly admitted Sister thus:

Esteemed Sister, the language of flowers has been studied and applied in all ages. The earth is vocal with the praises of God from unnumbered blossoms in vale and meadow, by the brook side and upon the mountains ; and these voices are heard and echoed in the hearts of all who in every nation have learned to adore Him. In our Society the graces of Jephthah's Daughter, Ruth, Esther, Martha and Electa are inculcated by means of emblems selected from the fields of nature.

The character of JEPHTHAH'S DAUGHTER is illustrated by the *Blue Violet.* This beautiful modest flower, in its bashful timidity, conceals itself amidst foliage from the face of the sun. Of the blue violet, the poet happily said:

I know thou art oft passed carelessly by,
And the hue so soft of thine azure eye
Gleams unseen, unsought, in its leafy bower,
While the heartless prefer some statelier flower,
That they eagerly cull, and when faded fling
Away with rude hand, as a worthless thing.
Not such is thy fate; not thy beauty's gift
Alone, bids thee from thy bower bereft: -
Not thy half-dosing, dewy and deep blue eye,
But the charm that does not with beauty die:
'Tis thy mild, soft fragrance makes thee so dear,
The loveliest gem of the floral year.

Such was the modest character of the Israelitish maiden, Jephthah's Daughter. Modest and bashful, shrinking from the gaze of' men, her life had been passed in the retirement of her father's dwelling until the sublime occasion called her forth which is so beautifully explained in our tradition.

The character of RUTH is illustrated by the *Sunflower*. This broad and stately blossom, which steadily faces the sun from his oriental to his occidental course, is an emblem of lofty and pure thought. As the poet expresses it:

Herein will I imitate the sun;
Who doth permit the base contagious clouds
To smother up his beauty from the world,
That when he please to be again himself,
Being wanted, he may be more wondered at
By breaking through the foul and ugly mists
Of vapors, that did seem to strangle him.

Such was the character of the Moabitish damsel, who came "from Moab's hills to Bethlehem's gates." In her days of prosperity, her wealth and rank had but gilded the bright purity of her soul, and in her poverty and desertion, when toiling, a poor gleaner in the fields of Boaz, the unalloyed graces of Ruth shone out with the halo of lofty and pure thoughts.

The *Sunflower* therefore is sacred to the memory of Ruth.

The character of ESTHER is illustrated by the *White Lily*. All nations agree in making this flower the emblem of purity, and its beauty and delicacy have ever been the theme of admiration from the time of Solomon to the present day. Even the Divine Saviour points to it with admiration, saying, "Behold the lilies of the field; . . . I say unto you that Solomon in all his glory was not arrayed like one of these." The poet has happily declared:

Fair white lilies having birth
In their native genial earth: -
These in sweet and queenly grace,

Match the maiden's form and face.

Such was the character of ESTHER, the matchless Queen of Persia, fairest among the women of the land, preeminent in intellectual gifts, the pride of the down-trodden people of God, exposed to all the temptations of pride, rank and a corrupt court, she still retained that purity of character which had elevated her at the first, and when the time of trial came, her heroism and self-devotion gained the favor of the King and saved her people from destruction.

The *White Lily,* therefore, is sacred to the memory of Esther.

The character of MARTHA is illustrated by a *Sprig of Pine.* This, in Masonry, reminds us of the immortality of the soul and the resurrection of the body, the two sublimest lessons the mind of man can contemplate. ·

The history of MARTHA as given in our traditions, is that of a young woman whose faith in Christ enabled her to resist the despondency that death had thrown around her, and to believe that her Brother should rise again under the Almighty Voice. Her faith was duly rewarded and her heart made happy in the reunion. The *Pine Sprig,* therefore, is sacred to the memory of MARTHA.

The character of ELECTA is illustrated by the *Red Rose.* In producing the rose, nature appears to have exhausted herself by her prodigality in attempting to create so fine a specimen of freshness, of beauty in form, of exquisite perfume, of brilliancy of color and of grace. The rose adorns the whole earth as the commonest of flowers. It is the emblem of all ages, the interpreter of all sentiments, it illustrates alike, our happiness and our sorrows. Its lessons are sung by the poet when he says:

'Tis not alone in the flush of mom,
In the cow-slip bell or the blossom-horn,
In noon's high hour or twilight's hush,
In the shadowy stream of the floweret's blush,
Or in aught that beautiful nature gives,
That the delicate *Spirit of Beauty* lives.

Oh no, it lives and breathes and lies
In a home more pure than the morning skies;
In *the innocent heart* it loves to dwell,
When it comes with a sigh or tear to tell,
Sweet visions that flow from the fount of love,
To mingle with all that is pure above.

Such was the character of ELECTA, combining all the meek domestic virtues with the highest and noblest heroism that is recorded in the books of history. In the pursuit of what she deemed Christian duty, she cheerfully surrendered all things, sealing the covenant she had made with her heart's blood.

The *Red Rose,* therefore, is sacred to the memory of ELECTA.

Choose, then, my esteemed Sister, which of these emblems, the Blue Violet, the Sunflower, the White Lily, the Pine Sprig, or the Red Rose you will adopt as yours.

The lady may have three months if she requests it, in which to make her selection. When made it is placed on record in the Book of Emblems, and can never afterwards be changed. The male members of the Family do not adopt Emblems.

Section 4

The affiliation of a member who has withdrawn from another Family, and .desires to unite with yours, is done in the following manner.

The form of petition is thus given :

To the officers and members of ············ Family, No.........:

The undersigned respectfully petitions to become a member of your Family. If approved, she (he) pledges herself (himself) to a cheerful obedience to all the requirements of the Family.

(Date)   (Name)
                    (One recommender)

This petition- must be accompanied by the fee, as stated on the Title page of the By-Laws. If from a female, it is handed by the Recorder to the Patroness, if from a male, to the Patron. They give it the same consideration as a petition for initiation (described in Section 2 of Chapter 3d) . Evidence in the form of letters of dismission and recommendation, proving that the applicant was a member of a Family in good standing, should be asked for. If this cannot be given, then reliable verbal evidence will suffice.

When the Patron has announced the acceptance of the applicant, the Conductress goes out and leads her in, taking her by the right hand. She conducts her to the Patron and introduces her in these words:

Enlightened Patron, It is my pleasant duty to introduce to you Mrs. (or Miss) A— B—, late a member of .... Family, No......... , who has been accepted as a member of this Family.

She brings with her an ardent affection for the teachings of the Eastern Star, and cherishes all the doctrines of the Order.

The Patron addresses the applicant as follows:

Esteemed Sister, welcome to our ranks. The recommendations you bring with you are amply sufficient to satisfy us that we shall find in you a worthy coadjutor in the work in which we are engaged. Welcome to our ranks. You will find us zealously pursuing the great ends sought for in the establishment of Adoptive Masonry. Welcome to our ranks. May the enjoyment and the advantages of your connection with us be reciprocal, and long and late be our parting.

The Patron then gives the signal for all to rise and addresses the Family as follows:

Officers and Members, Welcome our newly admitted Sister by the Family Hail.

The FAMILY HAIL. is then given by all present. The Patroness now goes forward and communicates the SOCIAL GRIP. Then the Conductress communicates the COUNTERSIGN, and the newly admitted member takes her seat at any convenient place. The Recorder is directed to enter in the Book of Emblems, the Emblem of her selection as recorded in the Book of Emblems in the F. from which she demitted.

If the applicant is a male the Conductor performs the ceremony of introducing him to the F. and he makes such slight alterations in the language of the introduction as may be necessary.

The following is a proper form of Diploma for a female member of the F.:

"We have seen His STAR IN THE EAST, and are come to Worship Him."

To All Advocates of Adoptive Masonry

This Diploma granted to Mrs. (or Miss) A---- B----, Witnesseth:

That our Sister is a member of .... Family, No .... ; that during her connection with us she has in all respects conformed to the requirements of the Family, and to the Laws and Regulations of the Order of the Eastern Star; and that we affectionately recommend her to the kindly offices and friendship of the advocates of Adoptive Masonry wherever she may reside or sojourn.

This should be located, dated and signed by the Patron, Patroness and Recorder. If the F. has a seal it should be fixed to the Diploma. Should the holder wish to use it as a traveling certificate, the signature of the Grand Patron, which can be secured without expense, should be added.

Section 5

The admission of visitors into the F. should be attended with such a display of courtesy as will gratify the visitor and endear her to her new acquaintances. It is done by the Conductress if the visitor is a female, by the Conductor if a male. Such evidence of the visitor's standing and identity should be demanded as the Patron may deem necessary.

When it is announced that a visitor is in waiting, the Conductress takes with her one other female member of the F., and goes out. They conduct the visitor in, the Conductress on her right and the other lady on her left, the three being hand in hand. Conducting her to the Patron, the Conductress addresses him as follows:

Enlightened Patron, It is my pleasant privilege to introduce to you, Mrs. (or Miss) A---- B----, a member of .... Family, No......... ,who has honored our Family with a visit.

The Patron then addresses the visitor as follows:

Esteemed Sister, We greet you with sincere pleasure and will endeavor to make your visit to us a pleasant one. Welcome to our Family.

The Patron then gives the signal for all to rise and addresses the F. as follows :

Sisters and Brethren! Make our guest welcome among you by the Family Hail.

All then unite in giving the FAMILY HAIL. The Patroness then communicates to the visitor the SOCIAL GRIP, and the Conductress communicates to her the COUNTERSIGN. After this she is escorted to a convenient seat. The Recorder is required to note upon his minutes the name and residence of the visitor. If the visitor is a male, member of the Family, the introduction is performed by the Conductor, assisted by some other male member of the Family, and such slight variations in the language of the introduction are made as may be necessary.

SECTION 6

The COUNTERSIGN is any one of the twenty-five words engraved around the border of the Membership Board. The Patron immediately after his installation (as described in Chapter 1, Section 10), selects one according to his own judgment, and communicates it to the members of the F. This remains as the peculiar COUNTERSIGN of that Family for twelve months, and must be promptly reported by the Reporter to the Grand Patron.

Description of the FAMILY HAIL and SOCIAL GRIP will be given in Manuscript.

The title of the Patron and Patroness is "Enlightened," that of others officers "Respected," and that of private members of the Family is "Esteemed."

CHAPTER FOURTH

THE BANQUET

SECTION 1

The Banquet being one of the most interesting portions of the business of a F., great attention should be paid to its preparation and management. *After the Banquet is regularly opened, visitors, both male and female, who have not taken the Degree of the E. S.,* may be admitted, if such be the will of the F., and it is recommended that such hospitality be frequently and abundantly dispensed.

The preparations for the Banquet are under the charge of the Treasurer and Watchman. The Treasurer will expend whatever sums in the preparation as the F. by previous vote, may designate, but it is recommended that economy in expenditures be used, and that the social element may the more abound. If preferred, the Banquet may be held alternately at the private residences of the members. This is recommended as a means of saving expenses to the Family and cultivating social harmony. As many members must be present at the Banquet as are necessary to work in the Family, viz.: 5 or more of each sex.

No particular shape of table is necessary. The Patron sits at the head, and the Conductor at the foot of the table. The Patroness is immediately on the left of the Patron, the Conductress immediately on the right of the Conductor. The Treasurer is on the right of the Patron half way down the table; the Recorder opposite to and facing the Treasurer. The other officers and members sit alternately around the table according to sex. Amongst the preparations, the following articles are essential:

1. Five letters cut from pasteboard, about an inch in height, each representing one of the initials * * * * *. These are laid on the table on the right side of the plates of the Patron, Patroness, Conductor and Conductress and Treasurer respectively.

2. Bouquets of flowers and hue as described in previous Chapters, to be placed on the left side of each plate.

3. Biscuits baked very dry and hard, cut in the form of a five-pointed Star, the whole about the size of a silver dollar. One of these is laid on each plate.

SECTION 2

The members of the Family and visitors who are members of other Families, being gathered about the table, and the door guarded against intrusion, the F. is then caused to rise by the proper signal and the Opening Service begins by the following invocation read by the Patron, or sung by the members:

Source of every earthly pleasure,
Bounteous Author of all good,
In Thy mercy's largest measure,
Bless this meeting and this food:
Grateful hearts will then adore Thee,
Grateful lives Thy mercy own,
Till in heaven we stand before Thee,
Till we worship by Thy Throne.

Then the officers holding up their respective cards (displaying the initials * * * * * repeat the explanations as follows:

Patron - *

Patroness - *

Conductor - * *

Conductress - * *

Treasurer - *

Then the other officers and members (not the visitors), commencing with the Recorder and going around on his left, hold up the Stars· (biscuits), and as each breaks off one point, she or he repeats the explanations as follows:

Recorder - Remember the Birth of Christ!

The next- Remember the Life of Christ!

The next - Remember the Death of Christ!

The next- Remember the Resurrection of Christ!

The next- Remember the Ascension of Christ!

Then all present, officers, members and visitors, hold up their bouquets and repeat the following invocations, the Patron leading the way and the rest responding in unison:

Break off a *blue* flower and repeat:

Blessed are the poor in spirit; for theirs is the Kingdom of Heaven!

Break off a *yellow* flower and repeat:

Blessed are the meek; for they shall inherit the earth!

Break off a *white* flower and repeat:

Blessed are the merciful; for they shall obtain mercy!

Break off a *green* sprig and repeat:

Blessed are the pure in heart; for they shall see God!

Break off a *red* flower and repeat:

Blessed are the peacemakers; for they shall be called the children of God!

Each one then gives the FAMILY HAIL., the Patron taking the lead, and then the Patron announces as follows:

Having thus observed the regulations of our Order, and opened our Banquet with appropriate ceremonies, let the doors be thrown widely open and our guests admitted to participate with us in whatever the Lord has provided.

If there are no visitors to enter, the Patron will use the following form of announcement instead of the above:

Having thus observed the regulations of our Order, and opened our Banquet with appropriate ceremonies, let us eat and drink whatever the Lord has provided us.

If visitors are waiting as provided above, they are conducted to the table by the Watchman and seated without ceremony. No signal to be seated is made here by the Patron, and none of the peculiar ceremonies of the Family are exhibited after the Opening.

Pleasant conversation, toasts, anecdotes, addresses, etc., form the intellectual repast, taking care however that nothing is said or done that infringes upon the secrets of the E. S., and that the strictest temperance be observed. Spirituous liquors must not be introduced at the Banquet.

At some period during the Banquet, as the Patron may designate, a contribution for charitable purposes should be taken up by the Treasurer.

Toward the close of the Banquet the five regular Toasts of the Family must be given. In these, the officers, members, and visitors from other Families participate.

Visitors who have not taken the Degree of the E. S. may remain, but take no part. The manner of offering these Toasts is as follows:

The Patron rises and repeats the first Toast, viz.:

Lasting honors to her- and whoever resembles her – who cheerfully resigned her life to vindicate the honor of her father!

All rise, break off a point from the star (biscuit) and eat it. All then take their seats.

The Patroness rises and repeats the second toast, viz.:

Lasting honors to her- and whoever resembles her – who cheerfully forsook home, friends, and all things, to make her abode among the people of God!

All rise, break off a point from the star (biscuit) and eat it. All then take their seats.

The Conductor rises and 'repeats the third toast, viz.:

Lasting honors to her - and whoever resembles her – who cheerfully forfeited her crown and kingdom to save the people of God!

All rise, break off a point from the star (biscuit) and eat it. All then take their seats.

The Conductress rises, repeats the fourth toast, viz.:

Lasting honor to her- and whoever resembles her – who cheerfully bore up amidst darkness, solitude, and death, nor for a moment lost her faith in the mercies of her Redeemer!

All rise, break off the last point of the star (biscuit) and eat it. All then take their seats.

The Treasurer then rises and repeats the fifth and last toast, viz:

Lasting honors to her-and whoever resembles her – who cheerfully gave her wealth, name, husband, children and life itself, as a testimony to her faith in the Lord Jesus Christ!

All rise, eat the central portion of the star (biscuit), and take their seats.

Between each of these toasts may be interspersed songs, speeches, and sentiments, at the discretion of the Patron.

There is no ceremony used at the closing of the Banquet but she or he retires at such time and in such manner as she or he may choose.

Chapter Fifth

Miscellaneous Directions

Section 1

The dates, etc., in the Recorder's Books of the F., must be kept in the Chronology of the Order, and all correspondence regulated by the same. To use this Chronology properly, write first the year, and then the number which expresses the number of days that have elapsed since the 31st of the preceding December. Thus: "1861, 97th Day," implies April 17, 1862; "1863, 310th Day," implies October 17, 1863, etc., etc.

Section 2

In the government of a F., the proper theory is that the Patron is responsible to the Grand Patron for the order and management of the proceedings, and for the due observance of all the laws and regulations of the Order. The granting of a Charter and the enrollment of a Family by the Grand Patron are predicated upon the pledge of the petitioners, and should the Patron of a Family so far forget his pledges as to allow any serious infringement upon the rules of the Order, the Family will be stricken from the rolls of the Order, and all other Families be notified to have no further intercourse with its members.

The Patron is responsible for the safe keeping of the Book of Instructions and Charter.

SECTION 3

Any officer or member of a Family may be allowed to peruse the *Book of Instructions* at the discretion of the Patron, and it is recommended that each one should have the opportunity of thus familiarizing themselves- their minds, with all the details of this beautiful system, whose symbolisms so strikingly illustrate the character and work of Christ.

SECTION 4

The only distinctive badge of office, additional to the ordinary Regalia of the Eastern Star, is a Rosette composed of ribbons of the five colors, blue, yellow, white, green and red, arranged tastily. This ribbon is worn by females on the left side of the collar; by males on the left lapel of the coat.

SECTION 5

All the expenses of the Family should be kept as much within bounds as possible, that so a larger donation may be given to the holy cause of charity, and the imputations of the world avoided. The necessary expenses of the Family are but trivial.

SECTION 6

No delay should be made in forwarding to the Grand Patron the names of ladies as they receive the Degree of E. S., and become members of the F. In all cases give the name with great precision, specifying the relationship she bears to Masonry, and the name of the gentleman through whom she bears it.

THE ROSARY
OF THE
EASTERN STAR

Synopsis of the System

Here is a story of the grand, old time,
A tale of virtues, tender, yet sublime,
Inscribed on sacred page to give us faith
In woman's constancy, in life and death:
Here, in God's book, the bright narration see,
And five brave hearts make up the history.

Adah, great Jephthah's daughter, soul of truth,
Ruth, flower of Moab, humble, pious Ruth,
Esther, the Crowned, and worthiest of a crown,
Martha, His friend, whom saints and angels own,
Electa, strong the martyr's cross to bear-
These are the heroines of the Eastern Star.

Fairest among ten thousand deathless names,
How altogether lovely do they glow I
Time's annals yield no brighter, nobler themes,
No purer hearts the ranks of heaven know;
Here, then, oh Sisters, sister-virtues trace,
And light from these your lamps of truth and grace.

In the recitation of these lines, a good effect is produced by the Lecturer taking in his left hand a pocket Bible and inserting the fingers of the right hand at the following passages, viz.: Judges, 11th Chapter; Ruth, 2d Chapter; Esther, 5th Chapter; John, 11th Chapter; 2d John, 1st Chapter. The application will then readily suggest itself.

The Landmarks
of the
Eastern Star

The following are the indispensable Rules, or Landmarks, under which the Order of the EASTERN STAR is disseminated:

LANDMARK FIRST. - The proper subjects for its reception are, Master Masons in good standing, (what is meant here by the words "good standing" is "not under charges, and not under discipline") and the wives, widows, sisters and daughters of such; but unmarried ladies, if under 18 years of age, are not entitled to receive it ; neither are half-sisters nor step-daughters.

LANDMARK SECOND. - The number present at its communication must not be less than five ladies, together with as many gentlemen as may be convenient. (To make this latter plainer, we add that Masons cannot even communicate this Degree to one another, save in the presence of ladies as above specified.)

Each person, before acquiring the knowledge of the Eastern Star must be honorably pledged to the observance of the above Landmarks, and to the strictest discretion in regard to the essential secrets of the Degree. Convenient forms for such pledges are given:

"So many of you ladies as do pledge the honor of a woman that you will not improperly divulge the secrets of this Degree, raise your right hands."

"So many of you gentlemen as do pledge the honor of a Master Mason to observe the regulations of this Degree, raise your right hands."

These requisitions being complied with, the Brother who is acting as Lecturer for the occasion (every Master Mason who has the right to receive the Eastern Star Degree has an equal right to communicate it, but only under the restrictions here specified) will proceed upon the general plan indicated in this volume; that is, he will make allusions, by way of opening, to the history, extent and purposes of Freemasonry; its claims to the respect and attachment of the ladies; and the practical objects for which the system of the EASTERN STAR was instituted. An Opening Ode of the Eastern Star may then be sung, as follows:

AN OPENING ODE

Air - "Just Before the Battle, Mother"

Here around the Altar meeting,
Where the Sons of Light combine,
Mingled with our friendly greeting
Is the glow of Love Divine;
For this Hall to virtue given,
And the Emblems on the wall,
Point surely to the Lodge in heaven,
And the MASTER of us all!

In the bonds of Masons' duty,
Seek we now the Master's Light,
Forms of Wisdom, Strength, and Beauty,
Teach us what is good and right;
Far be every sinful passion,
Near be every gentle grace;
And so at last this holy mission
Shall reveal our MASTER'S face.

The Opening Ode being sung, the presiding officer may recite the following lines of welcome:

A welcome and a greeting now,
To gentle friends and sisters true,
Around the place where Masons bow,
And pay their homage due;
On CHECKERED FLOOR, 'neath STARRY SKY,
Welcome sweet friends of Masonry!

To her who finds a FATHER here;
Or BROTHER'S strong and trusty hand;
To her who mourns the lost and dear,
Once cherished in our band;
To her who HUSBAND'S love doth own,
Greeting and welcome, every one!
Welcome the light our emblems shed;
Welcome the hopes yon volume gives -
Welcome the love our Covenants spread,
The wages each receives;
And when is past life's toilsome week,
Welcome the HOME that Masons seek!

The welcome having been recited, the presiding officer may open the lectures of the EASTERN STAR in the following or similar language:

The CROWN OF THE EASTERN STAR is made up of five chaplets, entitled JEPHTHAH'S DAUGHTER, RUTH, ESTHER, MARTHA, and ELECTA. We take from the Sacred Writings these five prominent female characters, illustrating as many Masonic virtues, and we adopt them into the fold of Masonry:

JEPHTHAH'S DAUGHTER, because she gave up her life through respect to the binding force of an oath.

RUTH, because she forsook all things through piety to God.

ESTHER, because she demonstrated by the heaviest sacrifices, her devotion to kindred and friends.

MARTHA, because she entertained undeviating Christian faith in the hour of trial.

ELECTA, because she exhibited the most perfect patience and submission under inhuman wrongs.

Following this, the Lecturer will pursue the line of instructions indicated in this volume, explaining the titles of the five Chapters respectively, and the use of the Scripture passages; reciting such of the Eastern Star poems as time and choice may suggest; singing the odes at discretion; and introducing the means of recognition of each part at a proper place.

It is recommended that from one to two hours be occupied in this pleasant manner. Alternating with the Lecturer's instructions the ladies themselves should be invited to communicate to and exchange with the gentlemen the various means of recognition, until it is shown that they have been perfectly acquired and understood. This is properly made a prominent part of the exercise.

THE FIVE CHAPLETS IN THE CROWN OF THE EASTERN STAR

My beloved spake and said unto me, Rise up my love, my fair one and come away.

For lo, the winter is past, the rain is over and gone.

The flowers appear on earth ; the time of the singing of birds is come, and the voice of the turtle is heard in our land.

The fig tree putteth forth her green figs, and the vines with the tender grape give a good smell. Arise my love, my fair one and come away.

The following are the flowers used as emblems in the Eastern Star. The colors are still further explained upon subsequent pages:

1. THE VIOLET- Its color BLUE, and its retired, shrinking nature are emblematic of JEPHTHAH'S DAUGHTER, the devoted Maid of Mizpah.

2. THE SUNFLOWER- Its color YELLOW, and strong, decided character are emblematic of RUTH, the pious Widow of Moab.

3. THE WHITE LILY- Its color WHITE and splendid bearing are emblematic of ESTHER, the noble-hearted Queen of Persia.

4. THE PINE LEAF- Its color GREEN and freedom from decay are emblematic of MARTHA, the Faithful Sister of Bethany.

5. THE RED ROSE- Its color RED and fervid character are emblematic of ELECTA, the martyred Wife of the Grand Master.

These lessons are combined in the following stanzas:

Culled from the plain and hill and valley
Grouped in mystic tie,
Ladies read me! sadness, gladness,
Every tongue have I;
VIOLET, SUNFLOWER, LILY WHITE,
PINE eternal, Rose delight

By the type of INNOCENCE,
By the type of PEACE,
By the WORD unbroken, spoken,
By the SUN of grace,
Judah's LION, emblems five,
Read me HIM and read to live!

The First Chaplet "F"
Jephthah's Daughter
The Tradition of the Veil

Lessons; The Mason's Daughter

Judges, XI Chapter

Color: Blue

Emblems: The Sword and Veil

Fairest of souls above,
Are those who suffered here;
They gave the sacrifice of Love
To prove their hearts sincere.

Historical Narrative

"And it came to pass, when he saw her, that he rent his clothes, and said, Alas! my daughter! thou hast brought me very low, and thou art one of them that trouble me; for I have opened my mouth unto the Lord and I cannot go back."- Judges, XI, 35.

The structure of Freemasonry, in its obligations, emblems, and principles, is so peculiar that we, Master Masons, above all other men, are taught to respect the binding force of an oath. The expression in the Book of Judges, "I have opened my mouth unto the Lord and I cannot go back," is recognized by us as expressing the highest duty of man. Perjury, to a Freemason, is the worst of crimes.

Therefore, when we find in Bible history, a person who submits to wrongs, to suffering and death, to secure the sanctity of an oath, we seize upon that character as our own. We adopt it. We hail it as a Masonic character and we claim whatever credit or honor may be associated with it.

Such a character, forcibly delineated, we discover in the Book of Judges under the title of JEPHTHAH'S DAUGHTER. And we have so surrounded the SACRIFICE of that noble and heroic woman with Masonic emblems, legends: and tokens of recognition as to make of it a section in what we call ADOPTIVE MASONRY. Therefore, whatever Mason's Wife, Sister, or Daughter justly emulates the character of JEPHTHAH'S DAUGHTER, she is our sister and our friend.

SUGGESTIVE LINES
JEPHTHAH'S DAUGHTER

She will not die as thief or murderer dies
Whose fate but expiates his horrid crime;
She will not veil her pure and loving eyes
As fearing death, for hers' is death sublime;
Lo, with determined heart and eye she stands,
Her face upturned toward Celestial lands!

The history of JEPHTHAH'S DAUGHTER, as composing a part of the EASTERN STAR, is thus given:

Her father, Jephthah, was a resident of Mizpah, in the mountains of Gilead, a warrior, and a man of decided personal character. He was a Freemason.

Being called upon in the extremity of his country's trials, to go at the head of its armies and resist the Ammonites, its enemies, he prepared his household for a campaign that would perhaps cost him his life, and then committed himself to the protection of God in solemn prayer. It was an age when religious knowledge was scanty and man knew but little of his Maker's will. Jephthah thought to propitiate Deity by a vow, such as his forefathers had made when about to depart upon dangerous enterprises. And this is the record of his vow as found in the XIth Chapter of the Book of Judges:

"Jephthah uttered all his words before the Lord in Mizpeh.

"And Jephthah vowed a vow unto the Lord, and said, If thou shalt without fail deliver the children of Ammon into mine hands,

"Then it shall be that whatsoever cometh forth of the doors of my house to meet me, when I return in peace from the children of Ammon, shall surely be the Lord's and I will OFFER IT UP FOR A BURNT OFFERING."

It is difficult to explain this vow. It has been conjectured that, being a hunter in the mountains of Gilead, Jephthah was accustomed to be much absent from home, and that on his return from those expeditions he was often welcomed by the favorite lamb of his daughter; and that this fact was in his mind suggesting the object of sacrifice, should his present dangerous enterprise be crowned with success. This explanation is accepted as the best at our command. Jephthah went forth to battle, expecting if victorious, to make a thank offering to God of the pet lamb of his daughter.

The victory was gained and the warrior returned to Mizpeh exulting in his success. God had redeemed his people. The thanks and praises of a grateful nation were showered upon his track. The loving father hastened home to enjoy the congratulations of his neighbors and still more of his daughter and only child.

Arriving upon the hill overlooking his dwelling, he halted. For now the full purport of his vow broke in upon his mind. The Lord had "without fail, delivered the children of Ammon into his hands;" he had "returned in peace to his house," and whatever "came forth of the doors of his house, to meet him, must be the Lord's to be offered up for a burnt-offering."

It was but for a moment. The door opened as his eye painfully regarded it. It opened and something came forth; not a pet lamb, not even a servant or a neighbor, but his daughter, his only child, the object in whom his very existence was bound up. "Behold," says the sacred narrative, "his daughter came out to meet him with timbrels and with dances." Jephthah rent his clothes and in the anguish of his heart cried aloud, "Alas, my daughter! thou hast brought me very low. I have opened my mouth to the Lord, and I cannot go back."

Adah was a daughter in every way. worthy of that warrior-sire, the mighty hunter of Gilead and the pious Freemason. Casting away the instruments of rejoicing, and changing the merry dance to more solemn measures, she answered, "My father, if thou hast opened thy mouth unto the Lord, do to me according to that which hath proceeded out of thy mouth." She had but one request to make and she was ready to be the sacrifice of the nation. She asked that she might go among the mountains for two months, and there, with the virgins of Israel, prepare her mind to meet in calmness and resignation, her impending doom. The request was granted, and during two revolving moons the heroic woman joined in the hymns and prayers of her friends, with which the mountain caves of Gilead became vocal.

The prescribed period being ended, the mournful procession returned to Mizpeh, where, in front of the home of her happy childhood, she met unflinchingly the fatal stroke that consigned her to perpetual honor and her friends to a life-long grief. Her father was the executioner of the heroic daughter, and her body was made a burnt offering according to his unhappy vow. For hundreds of years, and even down to the time of Samuel, "it was a custom in Israel that the daughters of Israel went yearly to lament the daughter of Jephthah the Gileadite four days in a year."

All this is communicated according to Masonic forms by emblems and ceremonies. The color BLUE recalls the cerulean hue of the mountains among which her pure spirit acquired that resignation which has been the wonder of all ages. The emblem of the SWORD recalls the instrument of her death. Mystical SIGNS, known only to the initiates, communicate important circumstances connected with her death, and a form of PASS is used to recall the lamentable but glorious event to which the entire history of Jephthah's Daughter refers.

THE CHRISTIAN APPLICATION OF THE FIRST CHAPLET

Although all Masons are not Christians, yet all the Christian virtues are Masonic ones. Whatever, therefore, will warm, move, enlighten and instruct the CHRISTIAN'S heart will equally affect the Masonic one; and this ROSARY would be strangely incomplete if, after bringing to bear all the Jewish exemplars of virtue and piety from the OLD TESTAMENT, we were to omit the no less impressive ones from the NEW. We shall, therefore, as has ever been done in the elucidation of this subject, bring the most striking analogies from the life of CHRIST to our aid.

The Christian Emblem appropriate to Jephthah's Daughter is the OPEN SCRIPTURES, and the motto is "the Word of God," For it was this that animated the heart of that young and devoted heroine in her premature death ; she believed there was a land beyond the river of death where youth is immortal and bloodshed is not known. Whence had she learned this? From the Word of God, recorded generations before by the great Law-giver, Moses. In her great sacrifice- vicarious, as redeeming the honor of her father before God- she foreshadowed HIM, "the Word made flesh," who should come so many generations later, and die a vicarious sacrifice for the sins of the whole world.

THE BLUE RAY

The color BLUE is appropriate to JEPHTHAH'S DAUGHTER. It alludes to the mountains of Gilead, among which was her romantic home at Mizpeh. Seen under the clear sky of Palestine, the ranges and peaks of the mountains are intensely BLUE, and this suggests the application of this color to Jephthah's Daughter.

The chaplet of flowers belonging to this department of the Eastern Star is made up of VIOLETS, selected on account of their color BLUE.

In the description of the Virtuous Woman given by Solomon the portions applicable to Adah are these: "Many DAUGHTERS have done virtuously but thou excellest them all."

The Second Chaplet "A"
Ruth
The Tradition of the Barley Parcels

Lessons: The Mason's Widow. Ruth, Chapters I to IV

Color: Yellow

Emblems: The Two Barley Parcels

> Among the ranks of earth
> Our noblest oft are hid ;
> But God will call His chosen forth,
> And crown the humble head.

Historical Narrative

Then said Boaz unto his servant that was set over the reapers, Whose damsel is this? — Ruth 11, 5.

The structure of Freemasonry, in its obligations, emblems, and principles, is so peculiar that we, Master Masons, above all men, are taught to respect devotion to religious principles. Upon our first entrance into the Masonic Lodge, we testify our faith and trust in God. We feel the force of that expression in the Book of Ruth, "Entreat me not to leave thee, or to return from following after thee; for whither thou goest, I will go; and where thou lodgest, I will lodge ; thy people shall be my people, and thy God, my God; where thou diest, will I die, and there will I be buried: the Lord do so to me, and more also, if aught but death part thee and me."

Atheism will effectually debar any person from becoming a Mason.

Therefore when we find in Bible history a person who forsakes houses, and lands, and parents, and country, through piety to God, we seize upon that character as our own. We adopt it. We hail it as a Masonic character, and we claim whatever credit or honor may be associated with it.

Such a character, forcibly delineated, we discover in the Book of Ruth under the title of RUTH. And we have so surrounded the PIETY of that noble and heroic woman with Masonic emblems, legends, and tokens of recognition, as to make of it a section in what we call ADOPTIVE MASONRY. Therefore, whatever Mason's Wife, Sister, or Daughter justly emulates the character of RUTH, she is our sister and our friend.

SUGGESTIVE LINES

RUTH

Pity the widow, desolate and poor;
Those little parcels are her only store;
Meekly upon her breast she crosses them
Prophetic of the Cross of Bethlehem;
Then looks, imploringly into the sky,
Where sits enthroned, the pitying Deity.

The history of RUTH as composing a part of the EASTERN STAR, is thus given:

Her husband, Mahlon, was a citizen of Bethlehem, who had taken up his residence in the land of Moab where he died. He was a Freemason.

Ruth was reared among an idolatrous people, whose forms and emblems of worship were more degrading, in a moral aspect, than those of almost any other race. She had been preserved· from the shame of Moab, and in becoming the wife of a pious and godly worshiper of the truth, soon acquired from him the knowledge and love of God. A few happy" years followed and then the calamity of widowhood came upon her. The record of her history is derived from the first Chapter of the Book of Ruth:

Elimelech and his wife Naomi, and his two sons Mahlon and Chilion, of Bethlehem-Judah, came into the country of Moab and continued there. And Elimelech died. And the two sons took them wives of the women of Moab, Orpah and Ruth, and they continued there ten years.

And Mahlon and Chilion died also, both of them.

Upon his death bed, Mahlon solemnly exhorted RUTH to leave that country after his death and seek one where the true religion of God was known. He warned her of the danger of losing the advantages she had already gained in the knowledge of spiritual truth, and told her of a people in the west, the nation of his fathers, to whom Jehovah had communicated His own holy mind and laws, and where she would find a sanctuary and a place of refuge. There he advised her to go and named the city of Bethlehem-Judah, as the place where his own ancestors had dwelt, and where God was.

Upon his death, she hastened to obey his behest, and with her mother-in-law, Naomi, took her desolate way from the land of her fathers. Although her sister Orpah returned to Moab, and Naomi herself discouraged RUTH from going to certain poverty and loneliness, she resolutely set her face westward delivering those beautiful words which in all ages have been made the medium of unreserved friendship and resignation.

"Entreat me not to leave thee or to return from following after thee; for whither thou goes I will go; and where thou lodgest, I will lodge; thy people shall be my people, and thy

God, my God: Where thou diest, I will die, and there will I be buried; the Lord do so to me, and more also, if aught but death part thee and me."

The sorrowing women went on foot to the city of Bethlehem and abode there. Pressed by poverty, RUTH betook herself to whatever honest employment presented itself, for their support, and it being the season of barley-harvest, she sought among the gleaners for that which the Mosaic law affords to all who are friendless and poor. It was her fortune to enter the field of Boaz, one of the wealthiest citizens of that place, and a Freemason. There she gleaned, by permission of the overseer, from early morning until the hour of high twelve, surrounded by the lowest off-scourings of Bethlehem, for the business of gleaning is confined to those persons who are fit for no other. The taunts of these wretches, their scornful jeers and the unconcealed ridicule of the reapers sunk deep into her soul, and overwhelmed her with mortification. The hot stubble pierced her feet; the scorching rays of the harvest sun of Palestine penetrated to her brain, and by the time the reapers had sat down to their noontide repast, Ruth had retired, exhausted and well-nigh fainting, to the friendly shade of a fig-tree where she reclined the image of loneliness and desolation. At this moment Boaz came into the field. Looking around he observed the unaccustomed sight, a gleaner, well-dressed, standing aloof from the noisy crowd, and presenting the appearance of one who had seen better days.

He inquired of the Overseer who she was; and received for answer the information given above, viz: that "she was a woman of Moab who had asked leave to glean among the sheaves, but being unaccustomed to the labor, had, in six hours, gathered only two little parcels of barley." This at once touched the heart of Boaz with compassion. He went to her, tendered her words of sympathy, and material aid, and then ordered the reapers to drop handfuls of barley on purpose in her way that so her day's labor might be amply compensated. The Sacred Narrative further informs us that he afterwards made her his wife, and she became the mother, through a long line of great men, of the Messiah, the Lord Jesus Christ.

All this is communicated according to Masonic forms, by emblems and ceremonies. The color, YELLOW, recalls the heated and golden stubble of the barley fields. The EMBLEM of the SHEAF recalls the incidents related of the generosity of the Freemason, Boaz. Mystical SIGNS, known only to the initiates, commemorate important circumstances connected with her history, and a form of PASS is used to recall the then lowering but afterwards glorious history of the heroic Ruth.

THE CHRISTIAN APPLICATION OF THE SECOND CHAPLET

The Christian Emblem appropriate to Ruth is "the Bunch of Lilies," and the motto "The Lily of the Valley," taken from Solomon's Song. Nothing could be more appropriate to the graceful and earnest spirit of that "Moabitish damsel." whose grand invocation, "Entreat me not to leave thee," floats down the tide of time with a power and melody all its own. As the lily is to its floral companions the type of beauty, modesty and humility, so is Ruth among women. As the lily among the thorns, so is Ruth among the daughters. Her fame shall grow as the lily and cast forth roots as Lebanon.

The analogy between the personal history of this heroic woman and that of the Redeemer of Israel is sufficiently exact for our purpose. That Ruth had been taught to put her faith in a coming Messiah may easily be supposed, when we recollect that the whole Jewish system of sacrifices, prayers and oaths, is founded upon that expectation. Every woman of the tribe of Judah hoped that her own son might be the "Shiloh that should come," and in her weary pilgrimage from Moab to Bethlehem, Ruth was cheered and upheld by the hope of religious converse with those who had been trained up in this faith. Her homeless condition recalls that of Him who "had not a place where-on to lay His head;" her sufferings from the taunts and sneers of the gleaners, those of Him who, "when reviled, reviled not again;" her grand acceptance and reward at the hand of the God of the widow and the desolate, that of Him who is "in the heavenly places far above all principality, and power, and might, and dominion, and every name that is named, not only in this world but in that which is to come."

THE YELLOW RAY

The color YELLOW is appropriate to RUTH. It alludes to the golden hue of the barley fields in which Ruth was gleaning when she met with favor at the hands of Boaz. The Chaplet of flowers belonging to this department of the Eastern Star is made up of SUNFLOWERS, selected on account of their color, YELLOW. In the description of the Virtuous Woman, given by Solomon, the portions applicable to Ruth are these:

"Favor is deceitful and beauty is vain; but a woman that feareth the Lord, she shall be praised.

"Give her the FRUIT OF HER HANDS; and let her own works praise her in the gates."

The Third Chaplet "T"
Esther
The Tradition of the Crown, Robe and Sceptre

Lessons: The Mason's Wife. Esther, Chapters 1-10

Color: White

Emblems: The Crown, Robe and Sceptre

> Ten Thousand anxious thoughts,
> Do oft our prayers oppress;
> But He who reigns in heavenly courts
> Will surely hear and bless.

Historical Narrative

Then said the King unto her, What wilt thou, Queen Esther? and what is thy request? It shall be even given thee to the half of the kingdom. — Esther, V, 3.

The structure of Freemasonry in its obligations, emblems, and principles is so peculiar that we Master Masons, above all men, are taught to respect fidelity to kindred and friends. We are introduced into Freemasonry by a friend, vouched for by a friend, conducted by a friend. Friendly hands support us through life, close our eyes in death, and consign us tenderly to the bosom of mother earth. There is no offense in Masonry more degrading than a breach of friendship. Judas Iscariot is as much abhorred by Freemasons as he is by Christians. The great Masonic society represents a kindred, a chain whose links are indissolubly woven into each other, a building whose several parts fit together with Divine exactness. We bear each others' burdens. The distress of one is felt by all. If a brother is hungry we feed him; if he is naked we clothe him ; if he is in trouble we fly to his relief.

Therefore, when we find in Bible history, a person, exalted in station, rich in this world's goods, learned and beloved, who casts all these advantages aside in her fidelity to kindred and friends, we seize upon that character as our own. We adopt it. We hail it as a Masonic character, and we claim whatever credit or honor may be associated with it.

Such a character, forcibly delineated, we discover in the Book of Esther, under the title Esther.

And we have so surrounded the Offering Up of the noble and heroic woman with Masonic emblems, legends and tokens of recognition, as to make of it a Section in what we call Adoptive Masonry. Therefore, whatever Mason's Wife, Sister, or Daughter justly emulates the character of Esther she is our sister and our friend.

Suggestive Lines

Esther

Nobly she stands; a Queen: the glittering band
Mark of a royal state, beneath her hand:
She points the silken robe with peerless grace,
Pure as her soul and pallid as her face;
Then reaches to the Sceptre whence is drawn
The kingly pardon she has bravely won.

The history of Esther as composing a part of the Eastern Star, is thus given:

Her husband, Ahasuerus, otherwise termed Darius and Artaxerxes, was King of Persia, a monarch of vast power, a man faithful to his word, and devotedly attached to the queen-consort. He was a Freemason.

The heroine, Esther, was a Jewish girl, and in common with all her people at that time, born a slave. She had been tenderly and piously reared by her cousin Mordecai. Her matchless beauty first attracted the attention of the King; her virtues secured his love, but her wonderful genius gained his permanent admiration and respect. No woman has ever left behind her such a record of wisdom as Esther. It is a standing tradition among her people that as Solomon was to men, so was Esther to women, the wisest of her sex. The more intimately the King became acquainted with her mental powers the more he respected them. There was no problem of state so intricate that she could not solve it. She became his confidant, and sat side by side with him, his equal on the throne of the kingdom. These circumstances enabled her in a season of peril to preserve her nation from destruction.

The enemies of the Jews, who were numerous and powerful, had brought false accusations before the King and persuaded him to utter an edict that upon a fixed day the entire race should be exterminated. The chosen people of God were doomed to be blotted from the face of the earth. The instrument to avert so great a calamity was the heroine, Esther.

No sooner did she learn the fate in store for them than she promptly resolved to save them or perish in the same destruction. The King had often admitted his indebtedness to her counsels, and pledged his royal word to grant her any request she might make him, even "to the half of his kingdom," and Esther now resolved to test his sincerity, and appeal to him, even at the risk of her own life, to reverse the horrible edict. She attired herself in her white silken robes, placed the crown of pearls upon her head, gathered her maidens around her, and went boldly and in state to the palace of the King at Shushan.

It was a day of Grand Council, a gathering of the governors, princes and officers of Persia. The dependent nations, to the number of one hundred and twenty-seven, had sent in their deputations to pay homage and tribute, and the royal guards thronged the ante-chambers of the palace. It was a standing law of that palace that none should enter the King's presence without summons, under penalty of death, and the sentinels as she passed reminded the Queen of this and warned her of her danger. But she bade them stand aside and so, pale but firm, she passed through the vestibule into the great Council Chamber.

The scene was magnificent, beyond the power of language to describe. The King, up in his throne of gold and ivory; the gorgeous equipages of his officers, and the splendor of the apartment itself, all made up a display rarely equaled and never surpassed. Through all the crowds of courtier Esther boldly passed and amidst the deathly silence of the observers, stood up before the King. Pale with fasting and sleeplessness, but not with fear, her cheeks emulated the whiteness of her silken robes. She fastened her eye fearlessly upon the King who, angry at the violation of the law, frowned sternly upon her. It was the crisis of her life. The wise woman felt it to be so, and at once reminded him of his former pledge by a method understood between them. She saw his golden scepter bent towards her, and hastened to secure her pardon by coming forward, kneeling and laying her hand upon it. Graciously said the King, "What wilt thou, Queen Esther? and what is thy request? It shall be even given thee to the half of the kingdom." The admiring crowds applauded the generosity of their monarch, and as he placed her beside him on the throne, gave utterance to loud expressions of admiration at her beauty, discretion, and favor with the King.

The Sacred Narrative informs us of the consummate tact with which Esther pursued the advantage she had gained. She achieved a complete success and saved the nation, which, to this day, keeps an annual festival in her honor.

All this is communicated according to Masonic forms by emblems and ceremonies. The color, WHITE, recalls the queenly robes of silk worn by her in the King's presence on that memorable occasion. The EMBLEMS of the CROWN AND SCEPTRE recall other incidents connected with the events described. Mystical signs, known only to the initiates, commemorate important circumstances of her history, and a form of PASS is used to recall the grand sacrifice and triumphant success of the heroic Esther.

THE CHRISTIAN APPLICATION OF THE THIRD CHAPLET

The Christian Emblem appropriate to Esther is the "Sun" and the motto is "the Sun of Righteousness," taken from Malachi, IV, 2. The figure of an effulgent sun is a royal type, a symbol of a crowned majesty, representing whatever sheds forth uncommon luster, whether moral or physical, to the world.

Thus it is emphatically an emblem of Esther, whose absolute fearlessness and devotion to her friends have sent a halo of glory through the twenty-four centuries that have elapsed since the world first felt the power of her example.

Pointing in this way to One who is the Source of all Spiritual Light, the Lord Jesus Christ, the history of Esther gains peculiar interest. The preservation of God's people was the preservation of HIS LAW, of the Divine traditions, of that thesaurus of hopes beyond the grave, found nowhere else but in the Bible. The sacrifice of Esther thus prefigures that of Him who fulfilled all these types, changed faith into sight, and hope into fruition, and removed the last veil that hides the face of a reconciled God from man.

It is not absolutely necessary to our purpose to suppose that Esther considered these things when she entered the King's palace on that memorable occasion, yet it is more than likely that she had been so trained up in the pious education of her childhood. To those, removed many centuries from her period, who rejoice in the tight of the "Sun of Righteousness" the following lines convey a wondrous fervor:

Great Sun of Righteousness arise:
Bless the dark world with heavenly light:
Thy Gospel makes the simple wise,
Thy LAWS are pure, thy JUDGMENT right!

THE WHITE RAY

The color WHITE is appropriate to ESTHER. It alludes to the royal robe of whitest silk worn by Esther when she entered the audience chamber to make known to the King her petition.

The Chaplet of flowers belonging to this department of the EASTERN STAR is made up of WHITE LILIES, selected on account of their color, WHITE. In the description of the Virtuous Woman given by Solomon, the portions applicable to Esther are these:

"The heart of her husband doth safely trust in her, so that he shall have no need of spoil. She will do him good and not evil all the days of her life. She maketh herself coverings of tapestry; her clothing is SILK and purple. Her husband is known in the gates, when he sitteth among the elders of the land. Strength and honor are her clothing; and she shall rejoice in time to come. She openeth her mouth with wisdom; and in her tongue is the law of kindness."

THE FOURTH CHAPLET "A"
MARTHA
THE TRADITION OF THE UPLIFTED HANDS

LESSONS: THE MASON'S SISTER. John, XI Chapter

Color: GREEN

Emblem: THE SHATTERED SHAFT AND GREEN SPRIG

And ALTOGETHER blest
Are those who know the Lord ;
The grave will kindly yield its guest,
To His resistless Word.

HISTORICAL NARRATIVE

And whosoever liveth and believeth in me shall never die. Believest thou this? — John XI, 26.

The structure of Freemasonry, in its obligations, emblems and principles is so peculiar that we Master Masons, above all other men, are taught to respect undeviating faith in the hour of trial. The great doctrines of Masonry are all borrowed from the Bible. Our devotion to Masonry is chiefly founded upon this, that we believe the Bible to be the Word of God, and therefore our principles, which are derived from the Bible were written by the finger of God. In this age and country a very large proportion of Masons equally believe that Jesus was the Son of God. One important branch of Masonry, the Templar Orders, illustrates the betrayal, sufferings, death and resurrection of

Jesus Christ, and all this in the most thrilling ceremonial ever beheld by human eyes.

Therefore, when we find in Bible history a person whose faith in the Redeemer was so fixed and thorough that even the death of her most beloved friend could not shake it, we seize upon that character as our own. We adopt it. We hail it as a Masonic character, and we claim whatever credit or honor may be associated with it.

Such a character, forcibly delineated, we discover in the Book of John, under the title of MARTHA. And we have so surrounded the appeal of that noble and heroic woman to her Saviour and her thorough confidence in His Omnipotent power, with Masonic emblems, legends and tokens of recognition, as to make of it a Section in what we call ADOPTIVE MASONRY. Therefore, whatever Mason's Wife, Sister, or Daughter justly emulates the character of Martha, she is our sister and our friend.

SUGGESTIVE LINES

MARTHA

Wildly her hands are joined in form of love,
As at the Saviour's feet the mourner lies; .
Beseechingly she raises them above,
While showers of tear-drops blind her languid eyes;
Then looks and pleads and supplicates His aid
In words that win her brother from the dead.

The history of Martha, as comprising a part of the EASTERN STAR is thus given:

Her brother, Lazarus, was a resident of Bethany, a man of good standing among his fellow citizens and the friend of Jesus Christ. He was a Freemason.

The family, composed of two sisters, Martha and Mary, with their brother Lazarus, seemed to have possessed all things needful for a happy life. Bound up in the love of each other and blessed with the friendship of Him whom (even now at this distant period) to know is "everlasting life," the little group were distinguished from their neighbors by a name that proved how thoroughly their hearts were occupied with Divine things. They were "the beloved of the Master, the happy household of Bethany."

Upon an occasion not described, when their Divine Guest had gone out, beyond the Jordan, upon a mission of charity, Lazarus was taken suddenly and violently ill. The terrified sisters hastened to inform Jesus of the fact by a messenger, who was instructed to say, "Lord, behold he whom thou lovest is sick!" They reasonably supposed that so tender a missive could not fail of success. But the Saviour returned an ambiguous reply. The "Beloved at Bethany" died and was buried. Four days passed, days shrouded with mourning, still the Saviour returned not.

The sisters were abandoned to grief, not alone for the loss of their brother, their only earthly protector, but for the unkindness of Him upon whom they had leaned as "the Rock of their salvation." Yet Martha retained her faith and trusted in Him yet to come and restore the friend they had lost.

At the close of the fourth day, intelligence reached them that Jesus was returning to Bethany; Martha hastened to meet him at the entrance to the village, fell on her knees before him, raised her hands imploringly towards his face, and with a voice almost suppressed with emotion, cried aloud, "Lord, if thou hadst been here my brother had not died!" Looking a moment after in his face, and animated by the god-like benignity with which he looked down upon her, she added those words which have rendered her faith a model to true believers in all the ages that have intervened: "But I know that even now whatsoever thou wilt ask of God, God will give it thee!"

Amazing faith! heroic spirit of confidence in her friend! Though her brother had been four days in the embraces of death and the subject of its corrupting influences - though the weight of watchfulness and sorrow rested heavily upon her spirit as she knelt there, her hands wildly raised to heaven - there was a spirit of prophecy in her words which give them a value all their own.

Then, said Jesus: "Thy brother shall rise again," testing her faith still further, and enquiring as to the extent of her confidence in his Divine power over death.

She replied: "I know that he shall rise again in the resurrection at the last day."

Jesus said unto her, "I AM THE RESURRECTION AND THE LIFE; he who believeth in me, though he were dead, yet shall he live; and whosoever liveth and believeth in me shall never die. Believest thou this?"

This test question met prompt reply. She said unto him, "Yea, Lord; I believe that thou art the Christ, the Son of God, which should come into the world."

The Sacred Narrative goes on in this moving strain, until the reader cannot forbear his tears. Mary next appears upon the scene, with the same tender rebuke, "Lord, if thou hadst been here, my brother had not died!" The three go next in mournful procession, accompanied by a crowd of spectators, to the grave of Lazarus. All were weeping; the disconsolate sisters, relatives, friends, townsmen, all who had felt the loss of friends or the sweetness of human sympathy, were alike dissolved in tears. Even the Divine One, whose own cruel death was impending upon the hill of Calvary, almost within sight from that little village, was melted into tears. JESUS WEPT! He wept tears of affection for Lazarus, tears of sympathy for the sisters, tears of compassion to those around.

Thus groaning in himself, and hand-in-hand with the sisters, he approached the sepulchre. Here the scene becomes awful beyond words to describe. "The Glory of God" was to be displayed by the power of the incarnate Son of God. A solemn prayer opened the stupendous drama, and then, with his own voice, as the voice of God, Jesus called forth the sleeping Brother, the hospitable house keeper, the faithful and devoted friend. And he that was dead came forth, bound hand and foot with grave clothes, and his face was bound about with a napkin. Jesus saith unto them, "Loose him and let him go."

All this is commemorated according to Masonic forms, by emblems and ceremonies. The color GREEN recalls the resurrection of Lazarus, and by direct inference that final and grander resurrection, when "the last trumpet, sending forth its miraculous blast through the sepulchres of the nations, shall call the dead, both small and great, before the throne."

Never does Freemason cast the evergreen sprig into the open grave of his brother but the coming event is thus beautifully foreshadowed. The EMBLEM of the BROKEN SHAFT betokens early death as in the case of Lazarus. Mythical SIGNS, known only to the initiates, commemorates important circumstances in the history we have detailed, and a form of PASS is used to recall the spirit of fidelity and trust in Jesus, which, above all other women, characterizes the history of the heroic Martha.

THE CHRISTIAN APPLICATION OF THE FOURTH
CHAPLET

The Christian Emblem appropriate to Martha is "the Lamb," and the motto is "the Lamb of God" from John 1, 20. The Lamb as it is the most tender, so it is the most expressive of all the emblems, both in the Jewish and Christian symbology. It is the very measure and mold of all the Masonic covenants, and is thus doubly worthy to be used in Adoptive Masonry.

The tender and affectionate Martha, equally devoted to her Divine Friend, whether as the grateful guest of the life-giving God, whether she was "cumbered with such serving" for his entertainment, or kneeling before him in the abandonment of sorrow, or walking with him weeping, to the sepulchre of her brother, is best represented under the guise of the meek and uncomplaining Lamb. "God has provided" her "a Lamb" for our delighted study. She is a Lamb "without blemish" in her display of womanly, social and Christian virtues, and she is one of those who are described in the latter books of Divine law as being "made white in the blood of the Lamb," and "written in the Lamb's book of life." To such as Martha are applicable the words following:

"Ye are come unto Mount Zion and unto the city of the living God, the heavenly Jerusalem, and to an innumerable company of angels, to the general assembly and church of the first born, which are written in heaven and to God, the judge of all, and to the spirits of just men made perfect, and to Jesus, the mediator of the new covenant, and to the blood of sprinkling that speaketh better things than that of Abel."

THE GREEN RAY

The color GREEN is appropriate to Martha. It alludes to the resurrection of her brother, Lazarus, from the sepulchre, where he had lain four days dead. It is everywhere used as the Masonic emblem of faith in the resurrection of the dead.

The chaplet of flowers belonging to this department of the Eastern Star is made up of PINE SPRIGS selected on account of their color GREEN.

In the description of the Virtuous Woman given by Solomon the portions appropriate to Martha are these:

"She considereth a field and buyeth it; with the fruit of her hands she planteth a vineyard.

"She perceiveth that her merchandise is good; her candle goeth not out by night.

"She layeth her hands to the spindle and her hands holdeth the distaff.

"She maketh fine linen and selleth it; and delivereth girdles unto the merchant.

"She seeketh wool and flax and worketh willingly with her hands."

The Fifth Chaplet "L"
Electa
The Tradition of the Martry's Cross

Lessons: The Christian-Martyr, The Wife of the Grand Master
2 John, I, 5

Color: Red

Emblems: The Enclasped Hands, Cup and Cross

Lovely upon the shore
Of Jordan's stream she stands,
Who gave her life for Christ and bore
His witness in her hands.

Historical Narrative

And now I beseech thee lady, not as though I wrote a new commandment unto thee, but that which we had from the beginning, that we love one another. 2nd John, I, 5.

The structure of Freemasonry in its obligations, emblems, and principles is so peculiar that we Master Masons, above all other men, are taught to respect patience and submission under wrong. That there will be a day of judgment, when all wrongs shall be redressed by Divine Hand, we firmly believe. As we view the matter, the six days of human life are days of toil, privations and trials of patience, all of which will be more than compensated to us in the Sabbath day of eternity.

Therefore, when we find in Bible history, a person whose confidence in God's justice gave her perfect patience and submission amidst the most inhuman wrongs, we seize upon that character as our own. We adopt it. We hail it as a Masonic character, and we claim whatever credit or honor may be associated with it.

Such a character, forcibly delineated, we discover in the traditions of our fathers; it is alluded to in the Second Epistle of John, under the title of ELECTA. And we have so surrounded the submission of that noble and heroic woman under wrong, her matchless generosity, and her patience as the hand-maid of the Lord, with Masonic emblems, legends and tokens of recognition, as to make of it a Section in what we call Adoptive Masonry. Therefore, whatever Mason's Wife, Sister, or Daughter justly emulates the character of Electa, she is our sister and our friend.

SUGGESTIVE LINES

ELECTA

Dying, as Jesus died, upon the tree
Was ever worthier sacrifice than hers?
Sacred the Cross, the nail, the thorn, for He
Who suffered has redeemed them from the curse:
Just as she passed to blest Eternity
She plead forgiveness to her murderers.

The history of Electa as composing a part of the EASTERN STAR, is thus given:

She was a lady of high repute in the land of Judea, of noble family, wealthy and accomplished, who lived in the days of St. John the Evangelist and was remarkable for her profuse benevolence to the poor. Her husband, named Gaius, was a distinguished Mason, formerly a Grand Master.

Electa had been reared, as all her neighbors were, a heathen. The idols of Rome were the only gods she knew. Like Ruth, however, she had been preserved from the abomination of the system, and when by good fortune she was enabled to hear from inspired lips the story of Calvary and its Divine victim, her heart readily opened to the influences of the Holy Spirit. She became converted, together with her husband and all her household. She even professed before the world her faith in the despised Nazarene, though well she knew that to do so was to expose herself to reproaches, to persecution, and haply to death.

Fourteen "Years, however, passed away before that great trial came upon her. Being the wife of so distinguished a Freemason, she enjoyed the protection of the invisible but potent shield of the mysterious Order. These years became the happier as well as the better years of her life. She gave her great income to the relief of the Lord's poor. Her splendid mansion was made a house of abode to weary and persecuted pilgrims. The poorest of the flock, the dusty, tattered, and footsore beggar, coming up the great avenue to her door was met as the father met his prodigal son. She ran out hastily to meet him, took him warmly by the hand, and "welcomed him in the name of the Lord." She led him to the best apartment, refreshed him with the richest wine in a golden cup, fed, cheered, clothed her guest, nor suffered him to depart until he was strengthened for the journey. Through all the country her name was famous as "the beneficent and affectionate Electa." And all this time she was ripening for the better world, and preparing for a fate which, although protracted, was inevitably to settle upon her.

Tradition has preserved the account of a visit paid to her by St. John, who, in the disguise of a beggar, came down from Jerusalem on foot to prove for himself the reports he had heard of her matchless hospitality. She met and led him into the house in the manner described. He said he was thirsty and a golden cup of princely wine crowned the board; ragged, and a suit of proper garment was given him; moneyless, and a purse was supplied with coins of silver and gold. He said he had no home and an apartment was prepared for him. Having tested his hostess in all these particulars, the sainted guest then spoke slightingly of "the new religion then noised about, called after a malefactor who had been crucified at Jerusalem some years before," and professed to wonder that any person could be deluded by so simple a snare. But the Christian predominated above the hostess, and she promptly bade him "cease or leave the house," for that "she was a Christian, as were all her household and the very entertainment that had been spread before him was prepared in the name and by the command of Jesus Christ, who had said, Inasmuch as ye do it unto the least of one of these ye do it unto me!" No further trial was needed, and St. John confessed himself outdone by the fidelity of his Christian sister.

But now the time of her martyrdom drew nigh. A great persecution began, and anyone who had confessed the name of Jesus was required to recant from his faith or suffer the penalty of the law. Electa was visited by a band of soldiers, whose chief officer, a Freemason, proposed the test of "casting a cross upon the ground and putting her foot upon it," whereupon he would report her recantation. She refused, and the family were cast into a dungeon, where they remained for a year. Their splendid mansion was destroyed by fire, and all their effects plundered and destroyed.

Then, the Roman Judge, himself a Freemason, came to the dungeon, and offered her another opportunity to recant, promising that if she would do so she would be taken under the protection of the Masonic fraternity. Again she refused, and this brought the drama to a speedy close. The whole family were scourged to the very verge of death. They were then drawn, on a cart by oxen, to the nearest hill and crucified. She saw her husband perish. She saw each of her sons and daughters die on the cruel tree. She was then nailed there, and being about to pass "to the better land," she prayed with her expiring breath, "Father, forgive them, for they know not what they do!"

All this is communicated according to Masonic forms by emblems and ceremonies. The color, RED, recalls the fervor of her hospitality, displayed in the ruby wine and the bountiful food spread before the poor and the needy at her table. The EMBLEMS of the Joined Hands, the Cross and Cup, recall incidents in her career such as those already described. Mystical signs, known only to the initiates, commemorate important circumstances of her history, and a form of PASS is used to recall the summing-up of the grand tragedy which crowned the life of the heroic Electa.

THE CHRISTIAN APPLICATION OF THE FIFTH CHAPLET

The Christian Emblem appropriate to Electa is "the Lion," and the motto is "the Lion of the Tribe of Judah" from Revelations V, 5. The allusion is to the almighty power of God, represented by the strength of the king of beasts. Nothing but this Divine power could have sustained Electa in those tremendous trials to which, for conscience' sake, she was subjected. The loss of good name; the loss of wealth and the means of doing good; the loss of liberty; the loss of husband and children; the loss of life-these were the successive trials to which the meek and lowly spirit was exposed, and it was only through the "Lion of the tribe of Judah" that help was derived "sufficient for her day."

Doubtless were the tender conferences of that gloomy dungeon recorded, they would read after this fashion, "For we know that if our earthly house of this tabernacle were dissolved, we have a building of God, a house not made with hands, eternal in the heavens." Such considerations, however, are not of human birth; they are suggestions of the "Lion of the tribe of Judah," the powerful One "who shall prevail."

Twelve hundred years after the death of Electa, a Christian poet, in a spirit almost of inspiration, breathed forth sentiments, in the Latin Ode, Dies Irae, worthy of Electa herself, some extracts from which shall close these histories:

"What then (in the Day of Judgment) shall I say, miserable sinner; which of the gods shall I invoke, seeing that the righteous scarcely shall be saved!

"Oh, King of tremendous majesty, Thou who doth freely save those who are saved, save me, oh Fountain of Holiness!

"Remember, oh, Immaculate One, that it was on my account Thou didst tread this lower earth, and let me not be lost in the fearful day!"

THE RED RAY

The color RED is appropriate to ELECTA. It is an emblem of fervency in the exercise of the moral virtues, and alludes to the admirable generosity of Electa, displayed particularly towards the poor and persecuted of her faith. The chaplet of flowers belonging particularly to this department is made up of RED ROSES, selected on account of their color, RED. In the description of the Virtuous Woman, given by Solomon, the portions applicable to Electa are these :

"She girdeth her loins with strength, and strengtheneth her arms.

"She is like the merchant's ships; she bringeth her food from afar.

"She riseth also while it is yet night, and giveth meat to her household; and a portion to her maidens.

"She stretcheth out her hand to the poor; yea she reacheth forth her hand to the needy.

"She is not afraid of the snow for her household; for all her household are clothed with SCARLET.

"She looketh well to the wants of her household and eateth not the bread of idleness.

"Her children rise up and call her blessed ; her husband also, and he praiseth her."

CLOSING ADDRESS

(The Five Degrees of the Eastern Star having been communicated, upon the plan indicated in the preceding pages, the Presiding Officer should rehearse, with much care, accuracy and repetition, all the MEANS of RECOGNITION, nor be satisfied to leave the subject until each of the ladies is thoroughly conversant with them, and each of the gentlemen able to recognize and respond to them. This being accomplished, the whole may be closed with this address:)

Thus I have gone the rounds of these five beautiful histories. You can now perceive how instructive are the Masonic traditions, when applied as they should be, to the Scriptures. Hear me, then, sum up the spirit of the whole subject. JEPHTHAH'S DAUGHTER, because she cheerfully rendered up her life to preserve her father's honor; RUTH, because she forsook "home, friends and wealth, that she might dwell with the people of God; ESTHER, because she was willing to resign her crown and life to save the people of God from death, or to perish with them; MARTHA, because, amidst sickness, death and loneliness, she never for a moment doubted the Saviour's power to raise the dead; ELECTA, because she joyfully rendered up home, husband, children, good name, and life itself, that she might testify to her Christian love by a martyr's death, find acceptance in all lodges searching for examples of endurance, fidelity and spotless honor. So, ladies, let it be with each of you. As you illustrate the virtues of these chosen and tried servants of God, so shall be your reward. You will not be called to suffer as they did, and yet sufferings and trials do await us all in this sublunary state; and those who, in the place to which they are called, best endure these trials, and resist temptations, prove that, had they lived in ancient times, they would not have been found wanting, though called to endure as a Ruth or an Electa.

One word more. As Freemasons, we earnestly solicit your good will and encouragement in the work in which we are engaged. I have proved to you that it is for your good as much as ours, that we are doing the Masonic work. Then, ladies, help us. Help us by defending our principles when you hear them attacked, and by speaking ever a kind word in our behalf. Your smiles and favor are the best encouragement we seek; with them we can do everything, and with them we pledge ourselves to do a double portion for you. And to those kind ladies who thus, while living, prove themselves the friends of Masons and Masonry, we promise that, living, we will love and respect you, and when you pass from this world to a better, we will remember you with tender regret and esteem.

GRAND CHAPTERS

NOT CONSTITUENT MEMBERS OF THE GENERAL
GRAND CHAPTER-1913-1914.

NEW JERSEY

Grand Matron, Mrs. Pauline Covington, Newark.
Grand Patron, William S. Smarzo, East Orange.
    Grand Secretary, Mrs. Margaret J. Bums, 15 Third St.,
    Weehawken.

NEW YORK

Grand Matron, Mrs. Lulu I. Hustleby, Niagara Falls.
Grand Patron, Dr. Calvin R. Moulton, Brooklyn.
    Grand Secretary, Mrs. Rebecca Niner, 25 West 42nd St.,
    New York.

SCOTLAND

Grand Matron, Mrs. Janet T. Cringle, Glasgow.
Grand Patron, Alexander F. Mennie, Glasgow.
Grand Secretary, Gilbert Gunn, 112 Bath St, Glasgow.

STATISTICS AND LIST OF OFFICERS OF
GENERAL GRAND CHAPTER

TABLE OF STATISTICS OF GRAND CHAPTERS, 1913
Which are Constituent Members of the General Grand Chapter

Grand Chapters	Organized	Month of meeting	Active Chapters	Active members
Alabama	March 6, 1901	November	114	3,468
Alberta	July 20, 1912	October	12	721
Arizona	November 15, 1900	February	15	1,279
Arkansas	October 2, 1876	November	249	9,225
British Columbia	July 21, 1912	June	10	797
California	May 8, 1873	October	285	35,940
Colorado	June 6, 1892	September	87	8,966
Connecticut	August 11, 1874	January	72	8,838
District of Columbia	April 30, 1896	January	15	3,544
Florida	June 7, 1904	May	63	2,696
Georgia	February 21, 1901	May	60	5,064
Idaho	April 17, 1902	June	38	2,655
Illinois	November 6, 1875	October	629	72,115
Indiana	May 6, 1874	April	307	28,165
Iowa	July 30, 1878	October	400	35,839
Kansas	October 18, 1878	May	311	24,836
Kentucky	June 10, 1903	October	178	9,558
Louisiana	October 4, 1900	June	9 1	4,752
Maine	August 24, 1892	May	162	18,487
Maryland	December 23, 1898	January	18	2,191
Massachusetts	December 11, 1876	May	131	20,581
Michigan	October 31, 1867	October	388	52,684
Minnesota	October 18, 1878	May	185	15,311
Mississippi	May 29, 1906	May	80	3,028
Missouri	October 13, 1875	September	366	26,594
Montana	September 25, 1890	September	57	5,210
Nebraska	June 22, 1875	May	204	16,343
Nevada	September 19, 1905	June	16	1,495
New Hampshire	May 12, 1891	September	47	5,762
New Mexico	April 11, 1902	October	35	1,992
North Carolina	May 20, 1905	June	54	1,524
North Dakota	June 14, 1894	June	72	5,712
Ohio	July 28, 1889	October	362	31,328
Oklahoma	February 14, 1902	May	210	13,199
Oregon	October 3, 1889	June	100	10,300
Pennsylvania	November 21, 1894	June	153	14,829
Rhode Island	August 22, 1895	October	12	2,072
South Carolina	June 1, 1907	June	51	2,148
South Dakota	July 10, 1889	June	111	9,097
Tennessee	October 18, 1900	January	138	6,000
Texas	May 5, 1884	October	540	30,325
Utah	September 20, 1905	May	10	1,093
Vermont	November 12, 1873	June	73	7,191
Virginia	June 22, 1904	May	34	2,035
Washington	June 12, 1889	June	138	13,402
West Virginia	June 28, 1904	October	62	4,625
Wisconsin	February 19, 1891	October	198	19,431
Wyoming	September 14, 1898	September	28	2,367
		Total	6,971	604,814

TABLE OF STATISTICS OF GRAND CHAPTERS, 1913
Which are not constituent Members of the General Grand Chapter

Grand Chapters	Organized	Month of meeting	Active Chapters	Active members
New Jersey	July 18, 1870	January	55	4,956
New York	November 31, 1870	October	485	47,561
Scotland	August 20, 1904	March	37	5,886
		Total	577	58,403

RECAPITULATION

33	Chapters under the immediate jurisdiction of the General Grand Chapter with membership of	2,029
6971	Chapters in the 48 Grand Chapters which are constituent members of the General Grand Chapter	604,814
577	Chapters in New Jersey, New York and Scotland	58,403
7581	Chapters, with a total membership of	665,246

ELECTIVE OFFICERS OF THE GENERAL GRAND CHAPTER SINCE ITS ORGANIZATION

	Most Worthy Grand Matron	Most Worthy Grand Patron
1876	Mrs. Elizabeth Butler, Chicago, Ill.	*Rev. John D. Vincil, St. Louis, Mo.
1878	*Mrs. Elmira Foley, Hannibal, Mo.	*Thomas M. Lamb, Worcester, Mass.
1880	*Mrs. Lorraine J. Pitkin, Chicago, Ill.	Willis Brown, Seneca, Kansas.
1883	Mrs. Jennie E. Mathews, Rockford, Iowa.	*Rollin C. Gaskill, Oakland, Calif.
1886	*Mrs. Mary A. Flint, San Juan, Calif.	*Jefferson S. Conover, Coldwater, Mich.
1889	*Mrs. Nettie Ransford, Indianapolis, Ind.	*Benjamin Lynds, St. Louis, Mo.
1892	Mrs. Mary C. Snedden, Wichita, Kans.	James R. Donnell, Conway, Ark.
1896	Mrs. Mary E. Partridge, Oakland, Calif.	*Nathaniel A. Gearhart, Duluth, Minn.
1898	Mrs. Hattie E. Ewing, Orange, Mass.	H. Harrison Hinds, Stanton, Mich.
1901	Mrs. Laura B. Hart, San Antonio, Texas.	L. Cabell Williamson, Washington, D. C.
1904	Mrs. Madeline B. Conkling, Checotah, Okla.	William F. Kuhn, Kansas City, Mo.
1907	Mrs. Ella S. Washburn, Racine, Wis.	William H. Norris, Manchester, Iowa.
1910	*Mrs. M. Alice Miller, El Reno, Okla.	Rev. Willis D. Engle, Indianapolis, Ind.
1913	Mrs. Rata A. Mills, Duke Center, Pa.	George A. Pettigrew, Sioux Falls, So. Dak.
1916	Mrs. Emma C. Ocobock, Hartford, Mich.	George M. Hyland, Portland, Ore.

	Right Worthy Associate Grand Matron	Right Worthy Associate Grand Patron
1876	Mrs. Mary A. Comstock, Indiana.	*Jeremiah E. Whitcher, California.
1876	Mrs. Lorraine J. Pitkin, Illinois.	Willis Brown, Kansas.
1880	Mrs. Ada A. Libbey, California.	*David B. Purington, Michigan.
1883	*Mrs. Lucinda Smith, New Jersey.	*B. R. Rose, Michigan.
1886	Mrs. Mary E. Mount, Nebraska.	*Benjamin Lynds, Missouri.
1889	Mrs. Mary C. Snedden, Kansas.	James R. Donnell, Arkansas.
1892	Mrs. Mary E. Partridge, California.	*H. Harrison Hinds, Michigan.
1895	Mrs. Hattie E. Ewing, Massachusetts.	*Nathaniel A. Gearhart, Minnesota.
1898	Mrs. Laura B. Hart, Texas.	L. Cabell Williamson, District of Columbia.
1901	Mrs. Madeline B. Conkling, Oklahoma.	William F. Kuhn, Missouri.
1907	Mrs. Ella S. Washburn, Wisconsin.	William H. Norris, Iowa.
1910	*Mrs. M. Alice Miller, Oklahoma.	Willis D. Engle, Indiana.
1913	Mrs. Rata A. Mills, Pennsylvania.	George A. Pettigrew, South Dakota.
1916	Mrs. Emma C. Ocobock, Michigan.	George M. Hyland, Oregon.
	Mrs. Ellie Lines Chapin, Pine Meadow, Conn.	Alfred C. McDaniel, M.D., San Antonio, Tex.

	Right Worthy Grand Secretary	Right Worthy Grand Treasurer
1876	Willis D. Engle, Indiana.	*John M. Mayhew, New Jersey.
1878	Willis D. Engle, Indiana.	*John M. Mayhew, New Jersey.
1880	Willis D. Engle, Indiana.	Mrs. Jennie E. Mathews, Iowa.
1883	Willis D. Engle, Indiana.	John R. Parson, Missouri.
1886	Willis D. Engle, Indiana.	John R. Parson, Missouri.
1889	Mrs. Lorraine J. Pitkin, Illinois.	*Mrs. Harriette A. Ercanbrack, Iowa.
1916		Mrs. Alcena Lamont, District of Columbia.

	Right Worthy Grand Conductress	Right Worthy Associate Grand Conductress
1895	*Mrs. Edna L. Hedges, Montana.	Mrs. Laura R. Hart, Texas.
1898	Mrs. Madeleine B. Conkling, Oregon.	Mrs. Ella S. Washburn, Wisconsin.
1901	Mrs. Ella S. Washburn, Wisconsin.	Mrs. Helen E. C. Balmer, Michigan.
1904	Mrs. M. Alice Miller, Oklahoma.	*Mrs. Rata A. Mills, Pennsylvania.
1907	*Mrs. Rata A. Mills, Pennsylvania.	Mrs. Emma C. Ocobock, Michigan.
1910	Mrs. Emma C. Ocobock, Michigan.	Mrs. Ellie Lines Chapin, Connecticut.
1913	Mrs. Ellie Lines Chapin, Connecticut.	Mrs. Cora R. Franz, Florida.
1916	Mrs. Cora R. Franz, Jacksonville, Fla.	Mrs. Clara L. Henrich, Newport, Ky.

* Deceased.

119

120

A Brief History of the Order of the Eastern Star
by Charlotte O. Stember
6x9 Softcover 180 pages
ISBN 161342227X

Seeking Light
The Esoteric Heart of Freemasonry
by Michael R. Poll
6x9 Softcover & Hardcover 156 pages
ISBN 978-1-61342-257-1
ISBN (Hardcover) 978-1-61342-438-4

Measured Expectations
The Challenges of Today's Freemasonry
by Michael R. Poll
6x9 Softcover & Hardcover 178 pages
6x9 Softcover Large Print Edition 210 pages
ISBN 978-1-61342-294-6
ISBN (Hardcover) 978-1-61342-410-0
ISBN (Large Print) 979-8-88457-534-9

A Masonic Evolution
The New World of Freemasonry
by Michael R. Poll
6x9 Softcover & Hardcover 160 pages
6x9 Softcover Large Print Edition 196 pages
ISBN 978-1-61342-315-8
ISBN (Hardcover) 978-1-61342-407-0
ISBN (Large Print) 979-8-32161-632-1

More Masonic Books from Cornerstone

An Encyclopedia of Freemasonry
by Albert Mackey
Revised by William J. Hughan and Edward L. Hawkins
Foreword by Michael R. Poll
8.5 x 11 Softcover 2 Volumes 960 pages
ISBN (Vol. 1) 978-1-61342-252-6
ISBN (Vol. 2) 978-1-61342-253-3

Masonic Enlightenment
The Philosophy, History and Wisdom of Freemasonry
Edited by Michael R. Poll
6x9 Softcover & Hardcover 240 pages
ISBN 978-1-61342-237-3
ISBN (Hardcover) 978-1-61342-426-1

The Freemasons Key
A Study of Masonic Symbolism
Edited by Michael R. Poll
6x9 Softcover & Hardcover 264 pages
ISBN 978-1-61342-228-1
ISBN (Hardcover) 978-1-61342-423-0

Our Stations and Places
Masonic Officer's Handbook
by Henry G. Meacham
Revised by Michael R. Poll
6x9 Softcover & Hardcover 178 pages
ISBN 978-1-61342-331-8
ISBN (Hardcover) 978-1-61342-697-5

Knights & Freemasons
The Birth of Modern Freemasonry
By Albert Pike & Albert Mackey
Edited by Michael R. Poll
Foreword by S. Brent Morris
6x9 Softcover & Hardcover 176 pages
ISBN 978-1-61342-150-5
ISBN (Hardcover) 978-1-61342-408-7

The Ancient and Accepted Scottish Rite in Thirty-Three Degrees
by Robert B. Folger
Introduction by Michael R. Poll
6x9 Softcover 2 Volumes 822 pages
ISBN (Vol. 1) 978-1-61342-240-3
ISBN (Vol. 2) 978-1-61342-241-0

Robert's Rules of Order: Masonic Edition
Revised by Michael R. Poll
6x9 Softcover & Hardcover 212 pages
ISBN 978-1-61342-231-1
ISBN (Hardcover) 978-1-61342-914-3

Masonic Words and Phrases
Edited by Michael R. Poll
6x9 Softcover & Hardcover 134 pages
ISBN 978-1-61342-167-3
ISBN (Hardcover) 978-1-61342-439-1

New Orleans Scottish Rite College

http://www.youtube.com/c/NewOrleansScottishRiteCollege

Clear, Easy to Watch
Scottish Rite and Craft Lodge
Video Education